TRAVELING THROUGH GRIEF

traveling
through
grief

LIFE, DEATH, &
TEN MONTHS
IN A TENT

CYNDI FRANCOIS

Beach Four
BOOKS

Traveling through Grief:
Life, Death, and Ten Months in a Tent
Copyright 2024, Cyndi Francois

Disclaimer: This book reflects the author's present recollections of experiences over time. Some names have been changed or details limited or modified to protect privacy. Other events were omitted, compressed, or fabricated, and dialogue has been recreated using journal entries, text messages, and memory.

ISBN (paperback): 979-8-9905210-0-1
ISBN (e-book): 979-8-9905210-1-8
Library of Congress Control Number: 2024908587

Edited by: Jocelyn Carbonara
Cover design by: Victoria Heath Silk
Book designed and typeset by: InsideStudio26.com
Proofread by: Amy Weinstein

Published by Beach Four Books, Bremerton, Washington

The life-changing journey after sudden and traumatic
loss is unlike any other human experience.
This is an attempt to capture it.

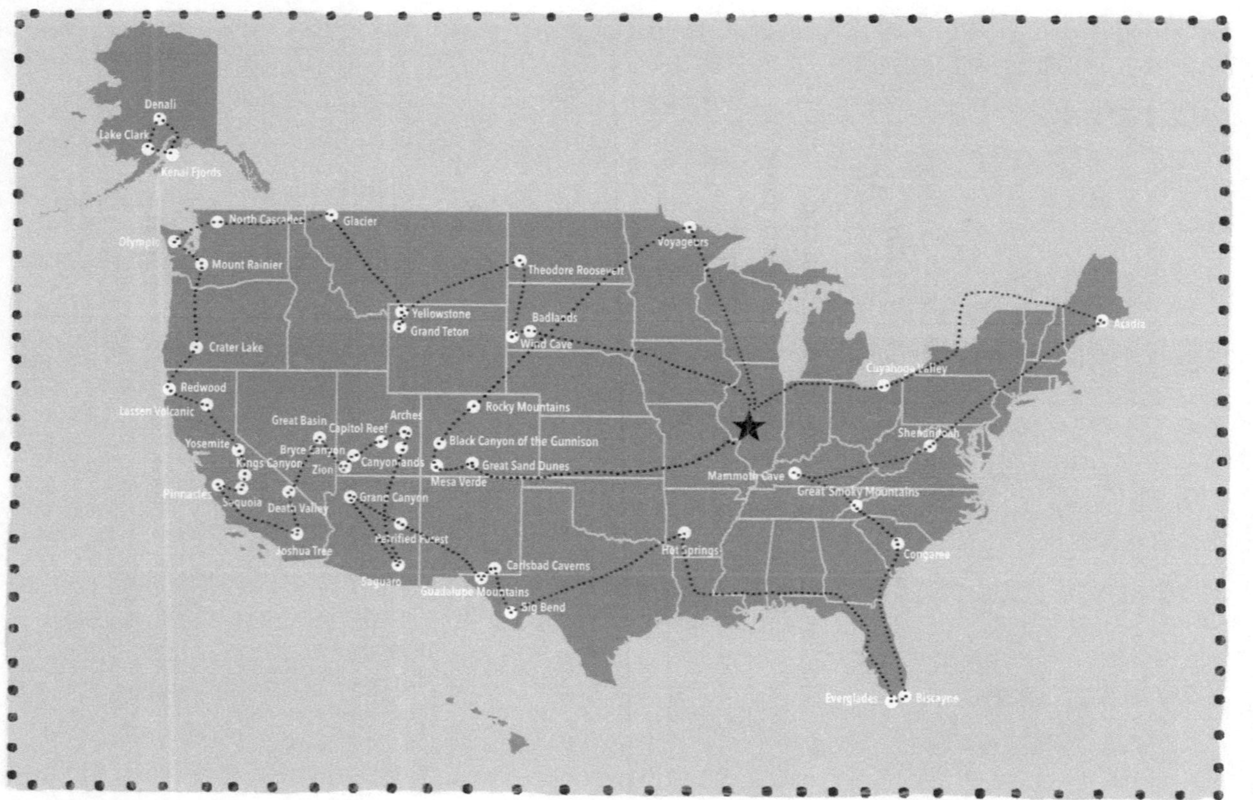

Denali
Lake Clark
Kenai Fjords
North Cascades
Glacier
Voyageurs
Olympic
Mount Rainier
Theodore Roosevelt
Yellowstone
Grand Teton
Badlands
Wind Cave
Acadia
Crater Lake
Cuyahoga Valley
Redwood
Rocky Mountains
Lassen Volcanic
Arches
Shenandoah
Great Basin
Capitol Reef
Yosemite
Bryce Canyon
Black Canyon of the Gunnison
Kings Canyon
Zion
Canyonlands
Great Sand Dunes
Mesa Verde
Mammoth Cave
Pinnacles
Sequoia
Death Valley
Grand Canyon
Great Smoky Mountains
Petrified Forest
Joshua Tree
Hot Springs
Congaree
Carlsbad Caverns
Saguaro
Guadalupe Mountains
Big Bend
Everglades
Biscayne

National Parks Visited, in Order:

1. Badlands, South Dakota
2. Wind Cave, South Dakota
3. Theodore Roosevelt, North Dakota
4. Yellowstone, Wyoming
5. Grand Teton, Wyoming
6. Glacier, Montana
7. North Cascades, Washington
8. Denali, Alaska
9. Kenai Fjords, Alaska
10. Lake Clark, Alaska
11. Olympic, Washington
12. Mount Rainier, Washington
13. Crater Lake, Oregon
14. Redwood, California
15. Lassen Volcanic, California
16. Yosemite, California
17. Kings Canyon, California
18. Sequoia, California
19. Pinnacles, California
20. Joshua Tree, California
21. Death Valley, California
22. Great Basin, Nevada
23. Zion, Utah
24. Bryce Canyon, Utah
25. Capitol Reef, Utah
26. Arches, Utah
27. Canyonlands, Utah
28. Saguaro, Arizona
29. Grand Canyon, Arizona
30. Petrified Forest, Arizona
31. Guadalupe Mountains, New Mexico
32. Carlsbad Caverns, New Mexico
33. Big Bend, Texas
34. Hot Springs, Arkansas
35. Everglades, Florida
36. Biscayne, Florida
37. Congaree, South Carolina
38. Great Smoky Mountains, Tennessee/North Carolina
39. Mammoth Cave, Kentucky
40. Shenandoah, Virginia
41. Acadia, Maine
42. Cuyahoga Valley, Ohio
43. Great Sand Dunes, Colorado
44. Mesa Verde, Colorado
45. Black Canyon of the Gunnison, Colorado
46. Rocky Mountain, Colorado
47. Voyageurs, Minnesota

Visited outside the trip:
48. Glacier Bay, Alaska
49. Gateway Arch, Missouri
50. Indiana Dunes, Indiana
51. Hawai'i Volcanoes, Hawai'i
52. Haleakalā, Hawai'i

prologue

AUGUST 3, 2018

A rumble of thunder jolted me awake. I glanced at my useless phone, which was just an expensive clock in this remote area. Its bright light pierced the pure darkness, temporarily blinding me.

2:33 in the morning.

No service.

I sighed and let my eyes adjust before realizing it was pouring rain—on me?

I hadn't thought we needed the tent rainfly. The dark sky had been glittering with a million stars when we fell asleep in South Dakota, exhausted from the long drive straight from Illinois through Wisconsin and Minnesota the day before.

Lesson number one on mountainside camping: always sleep with your rainfly up, no matter how beautiful or clear the night may seem.

I sprang to my feet and shook Shaun until he opened his eyes one by one—deeply confused, clearly sleeping heavier than I had in months.

After taking a minute to process what was happening, we ducked out of the tent, our eyes barely adjusting to the pitch-black night. We struggled to attach the rainfly, snapping at each other.

"Why didn't we put this up before we went to bed?" he asked, annoyed.

"I wanted to fall asleep under the stars."

I was embarrassed. I'd spent my entire life camping, but this was different. We were living out here now.

"Everyone else is still asleep," he pointed out, gesturing to the barely visible neighbors while he wrestled with the rainfly.

The rain droplets felt like small rocks pelting me from the sky. The powerful wind almost ripped the cheap material from our hands and blew it into the black abyss. A few frustrating minutes later, we finally secured the drenched roof to our tent and ran back inside.

The sides of the tent and rainfly flapped loudly in the wind, pushing and pulling in all directions. There was no way we'd be able to fall back asleep while listening to this.

Lesson number two on mountainside camping: a huge, floppy eight-person tent probably isn't the best choice on stormy nights.

What am I doing here? I thought to myself. *This is miserable. I'm miserable.*

I'd had visions of roaring campfires, writing in my journal beside the soft, warm glow of a lantern, cooking smoky meals on a cast-iron pan, falling asleep effortlessly after sundown, daytime naps in a hammock under trees, and a general isolation from society and life. I wanted to strip off the mask I'd been wearing, swim and bathe in streams and lakes, pick berries right off a hiking trail, and come face-to-face with wildlife.

My thoughts drifted. *The first night is never smooth. It won't always be like this.*

Our previous commotion had shifted the tent's contents up against its nylon walls. I gathered everything back into the middle of our shelter and peeled off my wet clothes, stealing a glance behind me to make sure Shaun wasn't looking. I quickly dried off my clammy body and squeezed the water from my long, tangled hair with a pair of underwear, the closest clean thing I could find.

I climbed into my damp sleeping bag, surrounded by puddles of standing water. My once-level sleeping spot was now slightly sloped, with my feet and legs resting just a bit higher than my head. I turned to my side, trying to adjust. A sharp pain shot right under my ribs; a large rock must have snuck itself under my thin sleeping pad. I tried to coax the stone out with no luck. Contorting my body until the rock was between my legs instead of my lower back, I settled in with a sad sigh. *Maybe this was a mistake.*

Everything was soaking wet. My light gray sweatpants absorbed the water through my sleeping bag, but I had no energy left to change again. I pulled the damp bag's cover over my head and spent the rest of the night sobbing into my water-logged pillow, replaying the last nine months in my head.

This memoir is a combination of journal entries (part I)
and travelogue narrative (parts II and III),
divided into the following sections:

I. The End
II. The Spiral
III. The Return

i. the end

you know the type of dread
when life is nothing but hell
your soul detached from
the body, a shell
eyes don't see
ears don't hear
tongues can't taste
voices won't speak
the lips forget
how to smile
fog takes over
it's dark
the end

NOVEMBER 13, 2017

Dear Wayne,

You died today.

You told me you were going to sleep for a few more hours before heading to work. You felt tired and had (what you thought was) some congestion or pent-up gas which led to broken sleep the night before.

That wasn't at all unusual for you. You slept in often, because you were a night owl and had a flexible work schedule. You felt sick for a few days but got better, and we had a great time at a wedding on Saturday. We were both hungover come Sunday. I drove us home a couple of hours from the hotel and stopped at Walgreens to buy you your favorite flavor of Gatorade—the teal one—but I grabbed the wrong one, because they had three different "flavors" of teal.

I spent the day on the couch with Icicle, our sleek black cat, and you spent it cuddling with Goose, our white fluffy cat, upstairs. I didn't see you much that day; we were both in and out of sleep and felt miserable. At around 9 p.m., you finally came downstairs. We ordered Rosati's, a Chicago staple. The *real* Chicago pizza—thin crust with a thick layer of cheese cut into squares, not deep dish (although we would never say no to a good deep dish). We always added a cheddar cheese topping with a side of ranch. We even splurged and got mozzarella sticks. We watched our shows while you cuddled and took pictures of the cats. This was our comfortable, familiar routine.

I should have known something was off when you only had one piece of pizza. But you said you just weren't very hungry. At around 11:30, you decided you wanted to go to bed early for work Monday morning. We said goodnight, and I watched you walk up the stairs to sleep in the second bedroom.

It was the last time I saw you alive.

The next morning, I was rushing around downstairs, getting ready for work. You were texting me from bed. "I just want to feel better," you wrote. "Come cuddle with me before your bohs dies." *Bohs, pronounced "hose" with a b, was our nickname, which I'd later get tattooed on my wrist.*

"Take your temperature and please go to the doctor, bohs. Especially if your chest hurts. I'm already late for work." I was trying to stay away from you in case you had something contagious.

"Good advice," you answered sarcastically.

We messaged about nonsense. Going grocery shopping. Getting gas. Normal stuff. I left in a hurry. "You left the hall light on," you said as I was pulling out of the garage. We messaged a bit more after I got to work, until you decided to take a nap. The last message you saw from me was at 9:44 a.m.

I sent you a picture of my lunch at noon, like always. But when I realized you still hadn't seen my texts, I started to worry.

I decided to let you sleep for a couple more hours. At one point, I asked, "Are you alive?" I didn't know it at the time...but you weren't.

At 2 p.m., I told my boss I was going to run home and check up on you and I'd be back in twenty minutes. But I never came back that day. And neither did you.

I felt it in my soul. Sitting at my desk, a deep, guttural sense of dread washed over my body. I had absolutely no reason to feel that way. You were feeling sick and told me you were sleeping. It had been about four hours since we last talked.

Why did I know you were dead? How could I know? Part of me had never been so sure of something in my life. The other part of me, the rational part, knew I'd walk in, wake you up, and you'd get up and go to work.

I stared at my phone the entire drive home. I was just waiting for you to message me when you were awake, so I could turn around and go back.

But you didn't.

I pulled into our driveway, ran up to the front door, and threw it open. The silence was loud. Not even your fan was on, and you always slept with a fan. Things felt…off. Wrong.

"Wayne?!"

The hall light was off.

That's a good sign, I reassured myself as I ran up the stairs, calling your name. You were the heaviest sleeper I had ever known. I didn't expect a response. But I also didn't expect what I saw next.

My husband, my best friend. The person who knew me better than I knew myself. This wasn't you; *this isn't real!* You don't sleep on your back. You're a stomach sleeper, like me. You rest your hand on your forehead, and you snore *really* loudly.

You were right there in the room with me, but you weren't. I touched your feet and legs. Ice cold. Hard. Your chest was lukewarm, almost taunting me, like there was still something I could do. I could hear my breath in my brain. I stumbled backward. The air was thick and suffocating.

Your eyes were closed, and your arms sat stiff against your body. Your lips and face were paler than I'd ever seen. Your phone was laying on the mattress next to you.

I slowly made my way to the window with the dark blackout curtain, walking diagonally. I was afraid to turn my back on you. I threw the curtains open, and the dim, filtered sunlight illuminated your body, highlighting the void in the room. I stared at you, we were both completely alone, completely frozen.

"We've only been married for six weeks!" I screamed at the 911 operator like it would bring you back. Maybe if I voiced the unfairness, the disbelief, that *no, this can't be happening*—maybe it wouldn't.

I did what I was told. I dragged your large, six-foot-four-inch frame from the bed to the floor. I will never forget the sound your body made when it hit the ground. Your head smacked hard against the dresser, because I couldn't support you all the way. I've never seen a body behave like that. Limp and heavy. I pumped your muscular chest. Too soft, too gentle. *Harder. Harder than you think.*

I tried beating life back into you. Maybe I could wake you up…maybe I could save you. *Yes! I won't stop until you wake up choking and coughing. Like the movies, right? Like how they tell us it'll happen! It happens all the time!*

I tried so hard, but it had been too long. Your hands and arms felt like plastic, and your face was white and glistening. I knew the second I stepped foot into the room I would fail. *Why am I even trying? I'm hurting you!* This wasn't the movies. This was actually happening.

No! We're not done yet. We have so many plans and so many dreams. You can't be dead! You had no idea. You would have said something. You would have called me. You aren't allowed to die on us! You're only twenty-seven. You're healthy. What about your family? Your sister, your mom, your grandparents, your friends. The cats. You can't leave us. We need you. I need you.

I waited with your body for the police and EMTs to arrive. It didn't take long—maybe four, five minutes—but time had stopped for me. I could have been standing there for hours and wouldn't have known the difference. The only thing that broke my trance was the doorbell, piercing the deafening nothingness. They ripped open the door and ran up the stairs, uninvited. *Maybe if they didn't come in, this wouldn't be real.* They ordered me downstairs while they worked on you. Asked a ton of questions I'm not even sure I answered. Searched our home. Wondered why you had boxes of latex gloves everywhere.

"He's OCD about germs," I whispered. For some reason, I felt like I needed to be quiet. I didn't want you to hear me. "He likes to be clean and careful."

A social worker called my parents while the police called your mom. And there I sat on the couch—in a daze, staring straight at the wall, in complete and utter shock while my brain fought and failed to process what had just happened. The strange woman put one hand on my leg and one on my back and looked at me like she had just seen a ghost. I suppose I looked the same.

Once our families got there, I was allowed to go back up and see you before they took you away in a body bag.

A *body bag!* You were taken from our home in a *body bag!*

I kneeled next to you and stared at your face. I kissed your lips and peeled back your eyelids, desperately trying to get one last look into your kind eyes, but they were glassy and fixed, resembling a doll's blank, chilling stare. My heart leapt into my throat, and I quickly closed them again.

"Ma'am, we're so sorry, but we're going to need to take the body now," one officer said. I pretended I didn't hear him. After all, I didn't, really. Your name is *Wayne*. Not "the body."

I kept staring at your blank, pale face, trying to memorize every freckle and every curve of your nose and cheeks while everyone watched in silence. A clear liquid dripped down the side of your closed mouth. I wiped it away with my fingers and brought them to my lips.

The EMTs knocked our framed engagement photo off the wall while navigating you down the stairs. I watched helplessly as you left our home—and my life—for the last time.

I still have the pizza box from our last night together. I kept the teal Gatorade I bought you—it has an inch of juice left. It was the last thing your lips touched. I touched my lips to its lid, over and over. I used your toothbrush. I used your deodorant and your cologne. I wanted you. I wanted to *be* you, so you could be alive, and I could be dead. I wanted to take your place.

NOVEMBER 14, 2017

Do you know what it's like to exist in silence? Everything is buzzing around you, but you're stuck. You're in some sort of glass case, and you're running out of oxygen by the second. It's hard to breathe. It's hard to move. It's hard to think.

You can't sleep. You can't eat. You can see life happening, but you can't *feel* it. Life has ceased in your little glass case. The grass directly under you is dead. The walls are fogged with your desperate, shallow breath. It's lonely. Silent. You beg for help, but nobody understands what you need.

Imagine if the birds stopped chirping. The sun stopped shining. Cars stopped driving. Politics and news channels abruptly ended. Your favorite TV series got canceled, your tastebuds stopped working, and words meant nothing. Things you used to enjoy are now painful reminders that make your body ache and your soul weep.

Six weeks after planning our wedding, I was planning my husband's funeral.

"You're so young," they all say. "You have your whole life ahead of you." I think they mean well, but I can't imagine feeling this tortured for a lifetime.

A new widow is consumed by primary and secondary losses. Like a chip left in a windshield from a rock, with its one deep gouge on impact. Over time, the crater starts to expand. Tiny cracks in the glass spider out, and if you don't repair them, they get deeper and harder to fix. The cracks keep spreading and eventually spiral out of control, affecting the integrity of the entire windshield. They never go away; the problem only gets worse.

How can it possibly get worse?

WAYNE

Wayne gave the best hugs; everyone agreed. He towered over everyone else, shy but confident, and my family nicknamed him *Tree*. His shiny, shaggy, brown hair got shorter as he got older, but that just exposed his long dark lashes and big brown eyes that lit up when he ate something really good.

His love for animals blossomed in college, and he got involved in environmental biology, hoping to work with them full time. We took each other to countless animal sanctuaries, wildlife refuges, rescues, and rehab zoos. We spent all ten of our birthdays and anniversaries doing something animal related, followed by dinner at a new restaurant.

He always chose the place after studying the menu to make sure they had a few of my favorite dishes.

"Eat it," he'd say, holding up his fork across the table. He always wanted me to try whatever he'd ordered. I'd narrow my eyes. He knew I hated seafood. "Boh, *no*," I'd answer in my most helpless voice. "I don't want it."

He would sit there all day if he could, staring at me until I caved. He'd rather his food go cold than have me refuse something he knew I'd end up liking anyway.

Food was a huge part of our lives. We drove for hours just to try a new place we'd seen on The Food Network or read about online. He made the most amazing chili and chicken wings and cooked most of our meals.

He took me to Broadway plays and musicals, introduced me to all my favorite music, and made sure we went to more concerts per year than I'd gone to combined before I met him. We had our own language and understood each other's moods with a simple look and snuck around to see each other every chance we got.

In college, I spent weekends visiting him, sleeping in my car around town because I didn't have anywhere else to go. My parents wanted me to stay and experience college life, and I just wanted to be with Wayne, so I didn't want them to know I was there. When I didn't drive to him, he'd surprise me at my dorm first thing in the morning after a last-minute, three-hour drive. We'd spend hours talking over cold shoestring cheese fries and soggy patty melts at Steak n' Shake, a Midwestern staple for broke college students looking for a place open 24/7.

We once sang the entirety of "99 Bottles of Beer" on a long road trip, promising never to do it again.

He was quiet, mysterious, and genuine. It took a lot to get him to open up to new people, but once he did, he was infectious. He cracked jokes softly under his breath that only I would hear, causing me to laugh at inappropriate times wherever we went. He was wonderfully witty, bringing me to tears and leaving my face sore.

He wrote me notes, drew me pictures, and gave me handmade cards for birthdays and holidays. He made up voices for our two cats, the loves of our lives. He picked specific songs to fit their personalities, creating self-titled playlists named "Goose" and "Icicle." He was smart and curious, always looking for the next adventure and always taking a lot of care and time while doing something.

He braided my hair in order to practice making braided enrichment toys for the animals he worked with at Brookfield

Zoo in Chicago. He adjusted my purse straps when they fell off my shoulder. He danced with me at every wedding we went to and made his younger sister a birthday lunch of spooky foods for her near-Halloween birthday.

He was meticulous and focused, sensitive and free.

Five months before his fifteen-year-old mother gave birth to him, his dad was killed by a drunk driver. His sister came eight years later, and he immediately took on a father-like role when her dad didn't want anything to do with them.

He was gentle and kind, not wanting to have kids of his own but patient with them anyway. He died with the same group of friends he grew up with, forming tight bonds that don't usually last through life's cycles.

He stuck his fingers down my throat one night after I got too drunk at a college party—after I cried in the bathroom because I couldn't do it myself and was terrified of puking. I made a mess, and he ordered me a sandwich and fed it to me on the floor until I passed out in his lap. He decorated my dorm door for my birthday, and he organized my bachelorette party because he knew me best.

He listened to music in the shower, belting out song after song. He always took his phone in the bathroom and put his playlists on shuffle. I never understood why his showers couldn't be quick and without music, but they were always longer than mine. I'd hear him through the bedroom and sing right along with him as I did my makeup at my beat-up vanity. He stayed in there until the water got ice cold, and I would suddenly hear shrieks and screams from the shock of the water rushing down his back; he never learned.

He would leave his hair in a ball on the shower wall. I always got so mad that he didn't just throw it away when he was done, but I would give anything to see that clump of hair in the shower again. He always bought Dove sensitive skin body wash, unscented. I thought it was so boring. Now, I refuse to empty the bottle.

He would use my blow dryer on the cold setting to dry off his entire body, because to only use a towel just wasn't good enough for him. He would come out of the bathroom completely naked, cleaning his ears with a Q-tip—just standing in the middle of the room so we could talk. He would turn the box fan on to further dry his body before he dared to put his clothes on. Some of the positions he got in for maximum airflow were impressive. Then he would carry his used towel by the very edge and hold it away from his body as he dropped it into the hamper, like it contained some sort of disease. He absolutely refused to use the same towel twice.

I miss his tiny beard hairs around the edge of the sink. The last ones he trimmed are still there.

We sang karaoke together and got pedicures and massages. He went to fancy hair salons and used expensive hair products but never once had an ego. His hands were large and soft despite his hands-on jobs and love for playing guitar.

"You never watch me play anymore," he would say sadly, strumming on the edge of the bed. "You used to be so engrossed."

"Yes, I do!" I answered with a twinge of guilt, because I knew he was right. His playing had become normal to me after a while—more background music than front row and center.

I supported him when his ten-dollar-an-hour seasonal position at the zoo was over, and he couldn't find another job. He supported me when I worked long hours at a male-dominated and toxic advertising agency—when I was tired, uninspired, sexually harassed by an "important asset to the team," and grossly underpaid, barely able to pay rent in my first dingy one-bedroom apartment I was so proud of. That apartment was eventually infested with bedbugs from a unit on the first floor, filled with carbon monoxide, and had neighbors with more cats than I would ever consider in a 500-square-foot area. It was a common occurrence to come home from work while the woman was scraping her overflowing litter box directly into the parking lot dumpster.

We were young—just seventeen and eighteen when we started dating—and things got hard. But we loved each other, and we knew it was all worth it. He did everything for me, and I did everything for him.

"You two were in your own world," a cousin told me. "Not disconnected from everyone else, but just completely immersed in each other. Your love was obvious and palpable."

We got married on a crisp autumn afternoon in a garden with colorful mums and fairy lights twinkling in the trees. At that point, we had loved each other for ten long years, and that day couldn't have been more perfect.

On the last day of our honeymoon in Costa Rica, we experienced a tropical storm. Stuck inside, we watched an episode of a show that featured a woman with a memorial tattoo that had her dad's ashes mixed into its ink.

"Would you ever do that for me?" I asked, slightly intrigued but also weirded (and grossed) out.

"Probably not," he replied as I hit him with my pillow. We laughed and ordered room service until we passed out.

Two weeks later, he was gone from my life, and I was convinced I wasn't going to make it.

NOVEMBER 15, 2017

I sat at the small, round table next to my parents and mother-in-law. The funeral director sitting in front of me slid a binder across the table, asking which casket I wanted to choose for Wayne. I didn't answer.

"You know, a lot of people like this option, because the inside material is more masculine," he said, probably to break the awkward silence in between my deafening sniffles and blank stare.

"I DON'T FUCKING CARE!" is what I wanted to yell. I wanted to scream it in his face. Over and over and over. I wanted to take that thick binder and smash it over his head. I wanted to rip up every page and price worksheet inside and light it on fire. Five days ago, my husband and I were eating pizza on the couch, and now he was dead, and I was being asked what kind of casket I wanted to rent for his dead body to be displayed in front of hundreds of people to gawk at one last time, wondering if he committed suicide, or overdosed on drugs, or did something reckless, because what healthy twenty-seven-year-old man just straight up dies?

He explained there were different types of woods, stains, and designs. The "masculine" padding inside had tufts with buttons, he said.

"The least expensive one," I choked out. It didn't matter. Nothing mattered. This went on for hours. Me, being expected to make rational decisions when I couldn't even see straight. My ears were ringing, and surely my head was stuffed with nothing but cotton.

We sat and planned Wayne's funeral like he and I had sat together and planned our wedding just six weeks before.

"Do you want a cross displayed in the casket with him?"

"Sure."

"Do you want one or two viewing days?"

"Whatever."

"Do you want a guestbook? What about memorial cards? Which photo do you want to use? Do you have a quote for the front? Which clothes do you want him to wear? Do you want him clean-shaven? Cremated or buried? Music? Photo slideshow?"

Stop him! Ican'tdothishe'snotdeadwhatarethesequestions?

Inside, my body was attacking itself. I couldn't breathe. I couldn't think. I couldn't move. I was sweating profusely. But somehow, on the outside, I managed to keep my composure. I answered all his questions. I signed on the dotted line.

I wouldn't remember much from those early days. I couldn't tell you who was at his funeral, or who was missing. I couldn't tell you what I was wearing, if I had eaten anything, or any of the well-meaning words people said to me. But I remember signing that dotted line.

I stared at the documents—stating Wayne's birth date, death date, and our relationship status. His entire life, summed up in this funeral home contract. I wanted to tell everyone he was so much more than that. Instead, I took the pen and looked around in disbelief. *Where am I? What the hell am I doing here?* This was the same funeral home Wayne's dad was displayed in twenty-seven years prior, before Wayne was even born. Talk about coming full circle.

After we left the funeral home, the decisions didn't stop. We had to pick out flowers. We were at the shop for what seemed like days. The woman across the counter kept asking what kind of flowers I liked. What I wanted for Wayne. She also mentioned masculine flowers. Is there such a thing? I wanted to tell her to fuck off too. Scream at the top of my lungs how little I cared. Just pick the damn flowers for me, so I didn't have to do this anymore.

Instead, I flipped robotically through the catalog. I thought about how convenient it would be if there were full-blown funeral planners like wedding planners. How stupid I was just a few weeks ago, being concerned about our wedding flowers and food. How pointless it all was.

NOVEMBER 17, 2017

It was my nephew's sixth birthday. One week before Thanksgiving and four days after I found Wayne's lifeless body in our home, I endured the first day of the two-day wake and services.

I got there early, after using every amount of energy I could muster to join my family in singing happy birthday to my nephew—smiling at him with dead eyes and ringing in my ears. *Happy birthday…*

I don't remember the car ride to the funeral home, but I can still feel the intense anxiety tightening my chest and loud silence piercing my ears.

The doors to the room where Wayne was lying were closed. Just two doors separated me from my husband's body. I hadn't seen him since 5:52 p.m. on the day he died in our home, where I wasn't even allowed to say my goodbyes alone because it was being treated as a possible crime scene.

After standing there for what felt like forever, I got the courage to walk inside the room. It's like I'd stepped into an alternate universe, one where absolutely nothing made sense, language wasn't understood, and time stood still. There were flowers everywhere; people had sent beautiful arrangements from all over. They smelled alive. I hated those flowers. *They shouldn't be here. I shouldn't be here. Wayne shouldn't be here. None of us should be here.*

I walked up to his open casket—slowly, holding my breath. I closed my eyes. I couldn't look at him. I hated myself, because I wanted to see him so badly. I wanted to erase the last image from my mind. I wanted to forget his ghostly-white pale skin. The slight sheen that covered it. The stiff, cold limbs I'd felt as I dragged him off the bed to try and give him CPR. The dead, blank stare in his eyes when I'd opened his eyelids in a panic.

I wanted to see him look like himself again.

Somehow, I got the courage to open one of my eyes. And then the next. My breath was literally taken away by the sight of him. I fell to my knees and gasped out loud.

This was not my Wayne. Maybe I didn't have a great perception of death. I'd only been to a few funerals, and the dead people mostly looked like themselves.

This is not my Wayne. What happened? Why does he look this way? I thought he would look better than this!

He was huge and bloated; his fingers were almost twice their normal size. His hands were placed so unnaturally over his oversized torso. He was covered in layers of foundation to hide his discolored skin. His neck was strained; he seemed so uncomfortable. He didn't look like he was peacefully asleep.

Because he wasn't. *He was dead.*

I wanted to reposition him myself, but I was terrified of touching him. My skin crawled with goosebumps and guilt, and I felt sick. This is someone I'd touched every day for the last ten years. I immediately took the snot-filled tissues out of my coat pocket and started wiping the caked-on makeup off his fingers and his ears. I rubbed furiously until the thick foundation looked even more messed up than before. His hair had some kind of product in it, which made him appear ten years older. I ran my fingers through it and tousled it the way he liked it. I touched his hands. He felt like a mannequin. Cold, hard, solid. Plastic. I couldn't do it anymore. I ran out of the room to my parents who were sitting in the kitchen area.

"He looks terrible! Why does he look like that?!" I screamed, collapsing into a chair at the table full of cold sandwiches and store-bought cookies.

The funeral director came over, kneeled down, and took my hands. With sad eyes, he explained to me that because of the autopsy and how long he was gone before I found him, things were going to be a little "off." They had to cut through his entire body to try to figure out what happened to him. He was sewn back together, and they put a shell on his chest. His head was propped up so we couldn't see his sliced-up neck.

I understood, but I didn't. I demanded they fix it. I didn't want anyone to see him this way. He wouldn't have wanted it!

The staff went into the room and took some makeup off; but when he looked the same, I gave up. I didn't have it in me to fight anymore. I walked back in and laid my head on his chest. I stroked his face. I leaned over his body and sobbed until my head was pounding so hard, I felt like he might be able to hear it.

It still felt weird to touch him, like he was going to come back alive and jump out and scare me any minute. He felt like the stuffed scarecrow my dad assembled with old newspaper and ratty clothes every Halloween.

"I love you," I whispered. "I know how sorry you are. The cats wish they could be here. I know you hate this as much as we do."

He would never want all that attention on himself.

"I wish I could have made this day more special for you, but I just can't. Please give me the strength to get through the next two days."

It was that day when I realized how resilient the human

body is. How much sorrow, grief, stress, and pain it can tolerate while you stand tall and keep going, because you have no other choice.

Somehow, I'd managed to walk to the podium at the front of the overflowing room. Every step felt like someone had poured one thousand pounds of wet sand into my shoes. It was like I had walked through wet concrete that immediately dried around my feet and legs, anchoring me in place.

It was the largest room in the building, and it was bursting with friends and family, young and old. People I was sure Wayne would outlive. Old men who could barely walk or breathe. People who had multiple cancers. Accidents. Life-threatening health scares. Parents. Grandparents. Even great grandparents. Every seat was taken, and people were lined up along the side and back walls, spilling out the open door into the lobby.

I had written Wayne's eulogy late one night while sleep just wouldn't come, no matter how many sleeping aids I swallowed. I sat awake in my dad's bed at my parents' house with a dim night-light and blank screen. How could I sum up Wayne's life in a few long paragraphs? How could I get across his goofy personality and calm demeanor in just a couple of pages? How could I do justice to him when I could barely form a sentence of my own without crumbling from the energy it took just to hold a conversation?

I couldn't, and I didn't. But I did know him best, and I knew I needed to be the one who spoke on his behalf. I wrote down whatever memory came to me that night while alone in a bed that wasn't my own—surrounded by dark red walls that felt unnecessarily oppressive. *I could write a book about him,* I thought. *How can I button it up in a five-minute speech?*

I looked out into the audience, avoiding the open casket to the left. I could still see it through my peripherals. My heartbeat tried ripping through my throat as my sweaty hands gripped the glossy printer paper. A piercing ring shot through my ears, and the muffled shuffle of life faded into the background, highlighting my shallow, shaky breaths. *I can do this. For Wayne. For Wayne. For Wayne.*

> Thank you for coming to celebrate Wayne's amazing life. Right now, it seems impossible. How can I bring myself to celebrate a life that was unfairly cut so short? At this point, I feel nothing but agony. But when I force myself to think about everything Wayne accomplished in just twenty-seven years, it brings tears of joy. He went to college, got his degree, worked with animals, traveled, got married, and had a home with loving pets.
>
> He has an amazing family who always supported him and loved him like they were his own son. His relationship with his sister was one-of-a-kind; even though they are eight years apart, they shared an unbreakable bond that I'm in awe of. He loved his mom and grandparents endlessly and selflessly. He was surrounded by dozens of close friends, most of them from middle school and beyond. I've never seen anything like it. Most friends drift; instead, they just got closer.
>
> Not only did they get closer, but they embraced me like one of their own from the very beginning. And they keep embracing me today. Over the years, they, too, became my closest friends. Without them,

I don't know how I would have gotten through the last few days.

We've been spending a lot of time together during these long, lonely nights. There are ups and downs. One minute we are holding each other, crying, and wondering how we will live a life without Wayne, while the next minute there's smiles and laughter at a vivid memory—probably something involving pizza or late-night shenanigans. And that's how Wayne would have wanted to be remembered.

Everything was a big production with Wayne, in a good way. From his passion for animals and accomplishing his dream of working with them, to his foodie lifestyle and traveling the country and the world. But interestingly, what keeps coming up in my mind are the little things. We've all heard it; it's the little things in life. And I've always believed it. But I didn't really get it.

When we went out to breakfast, I would finish my meal before he even started, because he took so much time making the perfect pancake, egg, and ham sandwich. He would drive an hour just to eat at his favorite burger place on a random weekday. Any concert he wanted to go to, tickets were bought immediately—even if that meant he had six dollars in his bank account until payday. He made custom music playlists for every event we were having, whether it be camping, a long car ride, vacation, or even songs that reminded us of our cats.

These things may seem trivial, and at times, may have even annoyed me; but I'm telling you this because it means more than a hot pizza or rocking show. It's more than Wayne just being a fun, laid-back guy. He taught me so much. To live life to the fullest, even when I think I can't. To seize opportunities, because why not? To become a better, more caring person, because that's who he was. He didn't sacrifice the things he loved most for convenience. He didn't waste his time wondering about the worst-case scenario. He just…did. And we can all use a little lesson in doing.

You know someone has touched lives when people all over the world reach out to you, telling you what they remember about them. People he only knew from one interaction on social media, people he met on his trip to Europe, people who share the same music tastes. I am speechless at how many messages I've been getting that start with "I only met Wayne once" or "I didn't know him very well," only to go on to say the interaction they did have was so memorable and special. He was magnetic. I can honestly say I don't think there is one person on this Earth who didn't like Wayne.

It still doesn't feel real. A few months ago, I was writing my vows to him. Now, I'm saying my goodbyes. As much as it pains me to know we were married for only six short weeks, I am so grateful to be his wife.

I'm going to do my best to honor his life by living mine the way he would have wanted. It will take time, but I can only hope he'll be with me every step of the way, even if I can't feel it. He knew how loved and supported he was, and I need to keep reminding myself that even though I lost a part of me, I gained so much more over the last decade. It crushes me to think about all the future plans we had together, but it's my mission to accomplish them. I will go to Boston and eat at his favorite restaurants. I will go to Europe to see a Muse concert. I will listen to all the music he wanted me to check out. I will finish our shows on Netflix. I will tour Chicago and stop at every chicken wing place he spent hours researching for us. I will travel as much as we planned. I will have more fun and stop being so uptight. I will live my life for him.

I know it sounds cliché, but please hug your loved ones a little tighter. Don't bicker about things you won't remember in a week. Tomorrow is not promised to anyone, and if this tragedy has taught me anything, it's that he is gone, but he remains.

I glanced up from the tiny, blurry words. "Thank you," I choked out. My shaking vocabulary was hard to decipher. I hoped everyone could understand me, but most of all, I hoped Wayne could hear me.

JANUARY 2, 2018

Fifty days have passed since you died. They pass by slowly, and quickly, and they are full of confusion, anger, and denial. Fifty days of constant ruminating and intrusive thoughts. *Were you scared? Was it fast? Was it slow? Did it hurt? Did you know what was happening? Did you suffer? Were the cats in the room with you? Were you waiting for me to come save you? Did you know I loved you more than anyone?* And the most obvious, that still wasn't clear: *How did you die?*

It's all so overwhelming, so I found just getting by with the basics has to be enough. Water, food, broken sleep, and fresh air when I leave the bed. Step by step and day by day is the only way I've managed to exist. The holidays came and went, and it had taken me hours to make your favorite cornbread casserole for Thanksgiving. Brain fog feels like I'm moving in slow motion, and I spent half the time on the kitchen floor scrolling through photos crying rather than baking.

These cozy cats are the only reason I'm up at all during the day, and although they might not get fed until late afternoon, they're eating, and we're together. It's the only thing that matters at this point. I'm still alive, and so are they. Their deep purrs and warm cuddles help with the constant void. I know they miss you just as much as I do, because now, they fight over my lap instead of having one lap each to themselves.

We had started to drift off together on the couch when my phone rang. "*Salmonella Sandiego*," the medical examiner said hesitantly over the phone. "This one really got me. He was healthy. I just couldn't pinpoint it…it doesn't make a lot of sense." Even the doctors were stunned. "Usually, only those with severe autoimmune issues have trouble fighting salmonella to the point of death. But there was nothing on his record, and nothing I could find. This particular strain of salmonella comes from small turtles. We found it in his bloodstream. It infected some organs."

My heart sank even lower than it already was. Your wedding ring felt heavy around my neck on the special chain my mom and dad bought to hold it. "We went to Costa Rica for our honeymoon two weeks before he died," I said, slowly. "I have been so scared our honeymoon killed him. It's all my fault." I felt hysterical, but couldn't hold it back. The thought hadn't left my head, and voicing it made it very real and very terrifying.

"Oh, I am so sorry. The strain is from the United States," he added. Relief temporarily flooded my body, but strangely, I did not feel relieved.

"I'm officially marking it *bacterial myocarditis caused by salmonella* on the death certificate. His heart was inflamed. He probably got very tired, went to lay down, and experienced an arrhythmia that caused a sudden cardiac arrest." He paused. My shallow breaths were getting louder. "I couldn't stop thinking of him. I tested everything I could think of, and this was all we had. No drugs. He barely even had any caffeine in him. I'm so sorry," he repeated. "I have a son his age. He was so young. This is very rare."

"How long? How long was it in his body?" I demanded answers. I was sick of hearing how rare this was, and I wanted it to make sense. "How do we find out where he got it?" I *needed* to know how this happened. "He worked at zoos and with animals for years. Could he have had it long term?"

"Finding out could be impossible," he said carefully. "There are only about 420 deaths from salmonella per year in the United States, and they're mostly food related. He could have come into contact with turtles or been near their environment, or someone with a pet turtle with salmonella could have served him food in a restaurant. I would start there."

I hung up. The medical examiner's serious voice was replaced with exaggerated purrs and a ticking clock.

You were always so careful. Remember your stash of latex gloves? How could this happen to you? You were overly cautious from everything you learned as a biology major and working with animals in college. You covered the kitchen in plastic wrap when working with raw meat. You generated so much more laundry with your refusal to use a bath towel more than once. We ate the same things. We were always together. How did you get salmonella, while I didn't? Why weren't there any symptoms other than occasional diarrhea that started in September? Why didn't you purge it like most people? I don't think you touched any tiny turtles recently.

If you'd had normal symptoms of salmonella, like vomiting, bloody diarrhea, and stomach cramps, I'm sure we would have been more concerned. If the medical examiner doesn't truly believe it, maybe it's not true. If it was salmonella, why couldn't you fight it off? He must be wrong. Surely there's another explanation!

All the possible scenarios I thought might make a shred of sense still made more sense than this.

"Oh, wow," the woman from the local health department breathed when I called to report the salmonella. "He should have just gone to the doctor and gotten antibiotics. You really could have prevented that."

I'm sure she didn't mean to sound accusatory, but all I heard was: *How didn't you know? Why didn't you save him?*

JANUARY 10, 2018

I think sometimes I'm trying to be too normal. What does normal mean now, anyway? It no longer means Cyndi and Wayne, Wayne and Cyndi. Now it's just Cyndi. But…that's not normal for me. You were my normal, and I was yours.

Normal was constant contact all day, every day. It was laughing at one of your one-liners, complaining about something trivial, and telling you stories about my day. It was tagging one another in posts online just to make each other smile.

It was coming home from work knowing I'd get to enjoy yet another night of normal. Finishing a TV series. Celebrating whatever national food day it happened to be. Planning on making dinner but going out instead. Going to concerts. Taking turns driving.

It was finding random socks in the couch and under the coffee table and wondering how hard it was to walk a few feet to throw them into the washing machine. It was you telling me not to be so uptight about being a few minutes late to something. It was sitting on our spots on the couch and just…being in each other's presence.

We had it down. Systems. Routines. Procedures. These were the little things that make up someone's normal. Of course, there was more to us than this. But it's these small things that happen every single day on autopilot, and when they're suddenly removed from life, every day feels empty.

Now, my job is to find my *new* normal. I can't continue to pretend I'm the same person, because she isn't coming back. I'm used to putting my best foot forward in everything I do. I like to be right. I like to do things for myself; it used to give me a feeling of accomplishment. I'm competitive. Interestingly, this holds true for grieving too. I want to stop relying on people. I want to do it all myself…but I'm physically and mentally unable.

Isn't it ridiculous? *I want to be better at being sad.* I want to be a better wife and handle all the legal issues and cancel your responsibilities in a timely manner. I want to be efficient. And I'm mad at myself that I'm not. That I can't.

With grief comes invisibility. Helplessness. It takes the person you were and transforms you into something you never thought you'd be. The old me would never allow other people to fold my clothes. I would never expect my dad to drive an hour to replace a lightbulb and take me to the store. I would never let someone scoop litter boxes and clean cat puke from my floor. My house had to be spotless and smell like a field of wildflowers if anyone was coming over, or they wouldn't be allowed in. *Where did that woman go?*

Why am I here? Right now, I'm only an inconvenience and a burden to everyone around me. I've regressed. This is just another loss of self that nobody could possibly understand. I need to remind myself just getting out of bed in the morning is a huge accomplishment. I never thought anything could be this hard. I'm doing the best I can, and it has to be enough.

I just wish I could be anyone else. I wish I could be the couple together in the grocery store. The child waiting at the bus stop without a care in the world. The old woman, lonely without her husband, but at peace because her time isn't far off and she's hopeful she'll see him again soon. Eventually, I will have to leave my old life behind and try to move forward. While the pain is still too raw at this point, living my old life is impossible when the most important part of it is missing.

I live in the same house. I drive the same car. I sleep in the same bed. I eat the same food. I have the same pets. I listen to the same music. I take the same walks. I have the same family and friends. I do our same routines…only you're not there to share them with.

Everything is the same; but it's so painfully different. I'm clinging to the idea of my old life, even though rationally, I know it's impossible. The reality is that I will never see you again. You're never coming back through that door. I still can't even bring myself to move your backpack and pair of jeans from the kitchen table, where you left them. Your toothbrush is still next to mine; our last pizza box is still on the counter. Your chili is sitting in the fridge collecting mold day after day. I haven't changed the sheets, and your dirty clothes sit in your hamper so I can smell them and hold them.

When I see a happy couple, or birth announcements, or engagements, or marriages, or people celebrating anniversaries, or anything, I get so upset. I hate that everyone else is happy and I'm miserable. I hate that I lost that happiness and those milestones in my life, but everyone else gets to experience them. I want them to feel what I feel. I pity myself and don't know how to stop. It's an ugliness I don't recognize in myself.

So many intrusive thoughts. Last night, driving home from work, I just kept imagining how easy it would be to drive into the other lane or into a tree. How easy it would be to end this suffering. How relieving it would be to stop the depression, anxiety, and constant flashbacks in my head. And then I think of how disappointed you would be in me and how I promised you at your wake I would live for you, and the guilt comes rushing in.

When I got home today, I opened your closet and touched your clothes. I looked at some old things and found your two broken laptops and a digital camera. Some old photos. A collage I made for your college graduation party. I sat on the bedroom floor and cried until my legs fell asleep and my tears started burning.

Then I laid right where you died. I laid there for an hour, trying desperately to feel you, or smell you, or hear you. I laid in the exact position I found you in, yearning for some kind of connection. Hoping for some answers.

Your mom is bringing me your ashes tonight. It hit me the other day that we just abandoned you at the funeral home. You were just sitting in storage. She's also bringing me the lock of hair I had the funeral director cut for me. I cleared a spot on the bookshelf, and you will stay with me. I hope having you here in our house will bring me some type of comfort.

This feels so bittersweet. I want you here, physically with me. I want your living, breathing body on the couch next to me. Not your ashes and ground up bones on the top shelf of the bookcase. I want to run my fingers through your hair on your warm head. Not through the few strands of it that we saved in a plastic baggie.

JANUARY 13, 2018

You've been gone for two months. I'm such a mess, Wayne. I often wonder what you would say to me if you saw me like this. I think you would feel so helpless, because nobody can do or say anything to take this constant heartache away. I'm the walking dead among the living. I don't feel anything. I don't see anything. I don't hear anything.

People are constantly telling me how strong I am, but they don't see me. They aren't there when I wake up in the morning with physical pain in my stomach, trying to calm my thoughts enough to stand up and get ready for work. They aren't there when I lay in bed crying out to you. They aren't there on my drive to and from work when I'm blinded by stinging tears and can't even remember how I got to my destination.

They aren't there when I'm making the terrifying decision whether to look through your photos and videos, wondering if it will ruin or help my day.

They won't be there when I'm sobbing on the phone, trying to cancel your accounts, whispering, "My husband passed away and I need to cancel. Where can I send his death certificate?"

I get the robotic "I'm sorry for your loss" over and over.

My loss? Exactly which loss are you speaking of? The loss of my husband? Best friend? Partner in life? The loss of my better half? The loss of my happiness? The loss of my future? All my plans? My security? My intimate life? The loss of daily communication for ten years? The loss of inside jokes, my support system, the person who has known me since I was fifteen, understanding all my dreams, fears, accomplishments, and failures? The loss of the person who I loved and trusted more than anything on Earth?

But what are they supposed to say? What am I supposed to say?

JANUARY 26, 2018

Today I'm traveling alone for the first time, on my way to a widow grief retreat in Scottsdale. It feels like we were just doing this yesterday, on our way to paradise for our honeymoon. Just three short months ago, we were in Costa Rica.

And just a few hours ago, I was using a plastic spoon to scoop out some of your ashes from your urn into an empty glass probiotic bottle. Your body, in my kitchen, resorted to powder. Your beautiful hands. Your contagious smile. Your thick, soft hair. Your big eyes and full eyelashes. Your long legs and strong arms.

Dust.

But I have to take you with me. You'll go where I go. It was our dream to travel the world together, and I'll keep that dream alive forever. Every road I travel, every mountain I climb, every ocean I swim in. You'll be with me. I'll leave a part of you behind in the most beautiful places I can find.

I miss talking and laughing while waiting for TSA. I miss your iconic travel meal of steak, egg, and cheese bagel and hashbrown. I miss being able to go to the bathroom without losing my seat; now I'll have to juggle my luggage in the stall. I miss resting my head on your shoulder.

Now I'm sitting next to strangers, holding back tears, because being around everyone else just makes me feel lonelier. I need to feel you in the sun. The breeze. The canyons and the trees.

I walked into the open outdoor lobby of the sunny Scottsdale resort. I was staying with my cousin in Phoenix, so I wasn't on-site like the rest of the group, but it was clear why they chose Arizona for a bunch of depressed people. Already feeling like an outsider, I approached the conference room where the first day of the retreat began.

I scanned the full, partially empty, and open tables. Older people filled each seat, and the room was overwhelmingly and disproportionally full of women. My eyes darted across the room. I spotted an empty table in the back left. I lowered my head, looked at the ground, and walked swiftly, hoping nobody would notice me. Wayne had only been gone for a couple of months at this point, and I still wasn't sure how to act in situations like these. I never knew the reaction I was going to have when I spoke of him; it was different every time.

I settled into the dark corner, pleased with my secluded choice. I was the youngest person there by far. Everyone seemed at least twenty, thirty, or even forty years older. I don't know why I thought this would be any different than the local Grief Shares I attended, which had predominately older women. *Because usually, you don't become a widow at twenty-eight,* I reminded myself. Connecting with older widows had only made me feel even more alienated. I didn't belong anywhere—not in my friend group, not at my office, not with my family. And certainly not in a group of widows.

"Hey," a voice said, cutting off my self-pitying thoughts. "This is the presenters' table, but you can still sit here."

Embarrassed that my isolation had caused more problems than it solved, I started gathering my things. Sitting with the presenters was the last thing I meant to do. I wanted zero eyes on me.

"No, really. It's OK. You should stay." She was young and warm, and I wondered if she'd lost the love of her life too.

"OK," I replied meekly. I suddenly felt self-conscious of my appearance. I hadn't worn an ounce of makeup and barely had enough energy to brush my hair or teeth since Wayne died. Looking around at all the other women dressed up and laughing had me wondering what was wrong with me. Why couldn't I be like them?

More people made their way to my once-peaceful sanctuary. A man, a few more women. They all introduced themselves as speakers and part of the Life Reentry Institute. I simply nodded as I forgot each name immediately.

I'd found the Life Reentry Institute online in my quest for any type of relief from my grief. It was founded by a woman who had lost her husband many years prior and made it her life's mission to help others along their own devasting journeys. It promised to help people who felt stuck in a place between the life they'd left behind and the life they wished they had.

The Institute's mission—to correct the false misconception that grief is a process of indefinite mourning—intrigued me. I didn't know how it was possible to feel any other way than how I felt now. I wanted to find out. I needed the secret that all these people seemed to possess. I was here looking for validation that I wasn't alone in what seemed like indefinite mourning. I was interested in the neuroscience and cognitive behaviors of grief and how to process the overwhelming emotions that engulfed me during every waking (and sleeping) hour.

I wanted all the answers.

By the end of it, I didn't have all the answers. But I did have new tools and "words" to describe what I was feeling, and a new hope that maybe one day, I could be one of the laughing and well-taken care of widows standing around the tables, eager to meet new people and share my story.

It turns out I *was* the youngest attendee—with the most recent and raw loss—in the entire conference room. Part of me was bursting with the need to trauma dump to everyone in the room, but the other half of me still didn't feel like I belonged. I skipped out on the arranged mixers and dinners after the days-long seminar, retreating to my cousin's apartment in Phoenix to sit with my feelings.

FEBRUARY 19, 2018

Once upon a time, you wrote, "When I die, spread my ashes on pizza. (You don't have to eat it.)" I don't remember the conversation. I don't remember why you said it. But you did, and I knew I had to honor your wishes, even if it was just a sick joke at the time.

This past weekend was the third annual cabin trip with your friends. They invited me in your honor, which was both a humbling and hurtful experience. Friday night before I left, I opened your urn and spooned out some of your ashes again. It wasn't easier than the first time. It will never be easy to see you resorted to dust.

I stopped and bought a Home Run Inn sausage pizza, your favorite frozen pizza—there aren't many options for delivery where we stayed—and I carried you with me in the front seat.

After I got to the cabin and a couple of hours had gone by catching up with the guys, it was time. I cooked the pizza to a perfect golden brown with slightly burnt cheese, just how you like it. We stood around the kitchen table and told stories, remembered memories, and drank beers that one of the guys brewed specifically for you. We cheersed to you after every memory in between tears of laughter and grief.

I sprinkled your ashes on top. They resembled grated parmesan cheese.

Nobody knew what to do after that. I went into this process wondering what we would do with the pizza afterward. Throwing it into the garbage was simply not an option.

Someone finally broke the silence. "What do we do now?"

I glanced down at the table, not sure how to respond. You'd melted into the cheese, fully becoming one with the bubbling pie.

"I'm not gonna do it," someone piped up. "I can't."

I grabbed the half-broken pizza cutter. The thin, crispy crust pierced the silent room. Eight small pieces.

I chose the biggest slice.

"Is this a health hazard?" someone else breathed.

"It's just ground calcium. It's fine," I said, slightly amused at who had a problem with it and who didn't.

"You first," they all agreed. I took a breath and took a bite. I chewed slowly as I looked around the room. All eyes were on me. What were they waiting for?

By the end of it, half the pizza was gone, and a few of us connected with you in ways we never imagined. I desperately hoped your traits would become mine, that I could absorb you. I'd exude you from my pores.

I wasn't sure if I was crazy or if I just wanted to feel closer to you, but it felt right to taste you.

FEBRUARY 22, 2018

Grief is *dirty*.

It's being **OK** with an astronomical pile of laundry in the corner.

It's knowing that your house won't always be clean when someone drops by.

It's the clogged shower drain. The dirty litter boxes. The cat hair covering the carpet. The dishes piled up in the sink. The forgotten garbage cans outside on garbage day. The sheets that haven't been washed. The car that's filling up with junk.

It's the unwashed hair. The unbrushed teeth. The toothbrush that belonged to him that you sometimes use. The leggings that have been worn three days in a row. The dirt under your fingernails.

Grief is *lazy*.

It's forgotten bills. Missed meetings. Canceled plans. The empty gas tank.

Staying in bed all day. Not going to the grocery store for six months. Forgetting to eat. Too tired to cook.

It's the mail you never check. The accounts you haven't closed. The bill collectors you ignore. The license you keep forgetting to renew. The taxes being done by your dad.

It's the face without makeup. The hair growing out of control on your legs and armpits. The clothes you do wash that sit in the dryer for weeks.

Grief is *awkward.*

It's people looking down when they pass you in the hallway. It's not knowing what to say in big groups. It's trying to smile for photos when all you want to do is cry.

It's sobbing silently at your desk while sharing an office. It's not knowing how to answer, "How are you?"

It's telling a cashier "I'm fine," when you clearly have tear-streaked cheeks.

It's letting your hairstylist know that he died. Your doctors. Your dentist. Your neighbors. Retelling the same story again and again. Reliving the tragedy every single time.

It's talking too much. It's not saying anything at all.

It's the close friendships that slowly fade away. The forgotten inside jokes. The truth of how you're doing that pushes people away. They're scared of you. And you don't blame them.

Grief is irrational and rational *fear.*

It's coming home after dark, terrified you're going to get raped and killed. That some psychopath is waiting for you in your garage. You've lived alone before and loved it, but this is different. This time, they know your vulnerability.

It's your new fear of the dark. But you're also afraid of the white, flickering Christmas lights you put up for a soft nightlight; what if the house burns down while you're asleep?

It's the fear of alienation, even though all you want to do is isolate yourself.

It's the fear of finding his dead body over and over and over. Again. And again. Every time you walk by that room. It won't go away.

And it's when the fear gets so bad that eventually you

realize…you have no fears at all. That's by far the biggest fear.

Grief is *lonely*.

It's waking up to a silent house. Coming home to a silent house. Going to bed in a silent house.

It's looking over at his spot on the couch, empty. Reaching out to hold his hand, but all you have is nothing.

It's lying in the exact spot he died, desperately trying to make a connection with him.

It's having nobody to tell anything to. Messaging your friends and getting no response. Going from constant communication with them to absolutely nothing.

It's discovering new music he would have loved. Buying concert tickets for his favorite bands. Standing in a crowd of people, feeling completely alone.

It's being the only one of your coworkers without a significant other. Eating lunch alone at your desk because you have nothing to say to anyone.

It's sitting in a restaurant for the first time without him. Looking out the window at the falling snow from a table for one, with families all around you.

It's being around your loved ones. It's hanging out with friends. It's doing all these things without him by your side.

It's having nothing but cats to cuddle with.

Grief is *obsessive*.

It's never-ending research. How deadly is salmonella? What does dying feel like? What happens during the dying process? How fast? Did you know what was happening? Flashbacks. What-ifs. Guilt. Questions. Who. What. When. Where. Why. Why. Why. Why. Why.

HOW?

Grief is *anger*.

It's when people try to relate and tell you about their dead grandparents or dead dog. It's when people compare the death of your soulmate to a breakup with their boyfriend or a divorce with their spouse.

It's when people say, "At least you had ten years; some people never find love." It's when a close friend says, "At least you experienced it. I've been alone my whole life."

Can't I just sit with my feelings without hearing "at least"? At least…what? I should be grateful my husband died, because at least he once lived?

It's wondering why there are terrible people in this world who get to live and love, when the best person you've ever known is dead at twenty-seven.

It's the thought of a ruined future. A ruined life, for both of you. Death is the most final, permanent thing that happens to humans.

It's anger that there is no hope for a different outcome.

Grief is *beautiful*.

It's the signs he gives you to show he's always with you.

It's the people you meet who you would have never crossed paths with before. The bond you share with other young widows.

It's the spirituality that you would have never found. The curiosity of the universe, religion, and more. The relationships in your life that get stronger. The generosity you've never received before.

It's the newfound appreciation to live life to the fullest. To look death in the eye and no longer feel afraid.

It's the urge to travel and honor him. The new experiences that you may not have pursued.

Grief is *love*.

It's having so much love for someone and knowing that love has nowhere to go. It's every memory. Every experience. Every inside joke. Every look. Every touch. Every smile.

The more you love, the more you grieve. The stronger the

bond, the stronger the pain. The closer you were, the further away they feel.

It's a shared life, shared goals, and shared passions, gone in one breath. Where does that love go?

It gets dispersed. Throughout your entire body. Your skin. Your bones. Your heart. Your lungs. Your throat. Your stomach. Every part of your physical body aches with trapped love.

Grief is shame. Grief is normal. Grief is individual. Grief is unbearable. Grief is dark humor. Grief is silent. Grief is loud. Grief is profound. Grief is physical. Grief is emotional. Grief is social. Grief is isolation. Grief is a journey.

MARCH 29, 2018

"What the *hell* is this disgusting Smucker's Orange Marmalade-tasting bullshit?!"

Wayne was enraged. We were at our favorite Chinese restaurant, House of Szechwan in Des Plaines, Illinois, back in 2013. He liked mixing soy sauce with sweet and sour sauce to create his own dip for eggrolls and "goons," his word for crab rangoon.

Apparently after the last time we ate there, they switched his favorite sweet and sour sauce to something that resembled orange marmalade, and he was irrationally angrier than he should have been. After that day, every time we got Chinese, he would judge the restaurant based on what kind of sweet and sour sauce they had. If it was the disgusting orange marmalade, the place lost some credibility with him.

Today, to "celebrate" our six-month wedding anniversary, I took my parents to another one of our old favorites, MingHin. The eggrolls were served with the disgusting orange marmalade bullshit. Memories of all the times we judged places on their sweet and sour sauce came flooding back to me, both making me smile and stabbing me in the heart. I wanted to tell my parents the story of Smucker's Orange Marmalade, but I just didn't have it in me. It took me all day to have enough courage to go there. I didn't want to talk.

Halfway through the semi-silent meal, my mom tasted it. "Hmmm," she said. "This tastes like…"

"Smucker's Orange Marmalade?" I interrupted.

"YES!" she yelled.

OK, Wayne. I hear you.

I told them the story. We laughed and laughed as we remembered how quirky and particular Wayne was with his food. Shortly after, we left the restaurant and drove across the street to get my niece and nephew some things for their Easter baskets. There was a seasonal aisle in the middle of the store dedicated to Easter stuff. As we browsed the little baskets and sifted through jelly beans, chocolate bunnies, and plastic eggs, something was nagging at me. My gut felt funny and my skin tingled. I felt my intuition nudging me to turn around.

Disgusting Smucker's Orange Marmalade bullshit! Eye level to me and placed randomly on a neatly stacked display of Nutella. It didn't belong there. There was no reason for it to be there. Out of the fifty-thousand-plus items a grocery store sells, what were the chances of one lone Smucker's Orange Marmalade jar staring me in the face on the same night I couldn't stop thinking about it? Plus, who even buys this?

Chills and goosebumps ran through my body. Tears exploded from my eyes, and I screamed and pointed to show my parents. I pulled out my phone and snapped photos, not caring about the people watching me and wondering what the hell my problem was. Admittedly, I made a scene. The aisle where Smucker's belonged was across the entire store. This was not a coincidence.

When I get a sign from Wayne, it's an out-of-body experience. It's something I cannot explain to anyone. I feel it in my bones and in my heart that this is Wayne, confirming that he is still around and that he hears everything I say and do. This time, my parents felt it too.

We immediately bought the jar, and my dad displayed it on his computer desk, because we decided Wayne would never want that disgusting marmalade in his house.

MAY 21, 2018

The company I work for is moving to Florida. Almost six months to the day after Wayne's death, all local employees were told that we're closing our doors by December of this year. I'm losing the one consistent thing I have in my life. The one thing that has allowed me to keep my home and all the memories associated with it.

Loss, after loss, after loss, after loss. I feel so stupid that I felt such loyalty to come back to work three weeks after Wayne's death—seeing as I could barely get out of bed—on day five of no showering, with another layer of dry shampoo on my greasy scalp. I had no PTO from the wedding and honeymoon, no second income, nothing. I had to survive. I walked into work every single day, despite feeling like my world just possibly could not go on. I stayed the full eight hours, sometimes even more. I hit all my deadlines, despite tasks taking me astronomically longer than I was used to. I couldn't even bring myself to type an exclamation point in an email or message to my coworkers.

I only called off one morning due to my grief. And now they're taking away my job. And it has me terrified that my life and future is so unknown and bleak. Do I move to Florida? Is that even an option? Do I move in with my parents? Do I move to a different country or state, and completely start over? Do I just try and find another job near me so I can keep my home?

Problem is, all those options suck. Because Wayne is still dead. A job is just a job. And I'm still here, alone. Making these impossible decisions by myself. Where will I go? What will I do? Where will I live? Who will I be? What will I do with our stuff?

What about Wayne's clothes? Shoes? Jackets? Toothbrush? Hair products? Cologne? Books? Video games? Guitars? Memories? *His entire life.* How can I do this? The other day, it took me half an hour to mentally prepare to throw the chili in the fridge away. His prized dish. It was almost nine months old—and pretty much living. It was covered in pink, white, and green mold. All three containers of them. I let those containers sit and rot in the fridge for almost *nine months.* I couldn't bring myself to toss them out. They were in glass Pyrex containers— the ones we bought on Black Friday a few years ago. I tossed those too; I had no energy to clean the mess. It all went into the garbage and out of the house.

It's all too overwhelming. My fight or flight is more like a freeze, and I am stuck and directionless. I desperately want a "reset" button, something that will take me back to the basics. Help me rediscover what's important to me. My first instinct is to be alone, away from the triggers of my past.

I'll be alone for the rest of my life; might as well learn how now.

So I've decided to leave this life for a life on the road in August. Nature is pulling me in, and I'm listening. I want to be unbothered, completely immersed in something bigger than me. I crave simplicity, beauty, and isolation. I'm tired of putting on a mask every day. Tired of all the small talk, the dissociation, the things people complain about, and everything that doesn't matter. Tired of pretending to care about what used to excite me, and tired of acting like I've had a better day than the day that came before. I'm tired of trying to fit in; the pressure to not be a downer in group situations is crushing. I'm tired of the meaningless conversation that I used to take part in. I'm tired of this materialistic society, one that has no idea how to deal with grief or mental health.

"Did he smell? You know…when you found him?" one of my coworkers asked me a few weeks after returning to the office.

You see, I'm just tired, and I don't care if I come back.

I'm going to hit every national park in the lower forty-eight states on one long road trip, and I'll spread a portion of Wayne's ashes at each one in the most beautiful place I can find. Having been to many national parks together, using our vacation time to road trip and camp in the most beautiful and remote places in this country, it seems fitting. Things were so simple on those trips. Quick and cheap meals, minimal expenses, and miles of abandoned roads to reflect on.

My husband is dead, and I'm losing my home and job, all within six months. Life, as I knew it, is crumbling before my eyes. All I want to do is drive. Run away from everything I've become.

MAY 24, 2018

I read an article the other day that listed the top five most stressful situations in a human's life. Number one: death of a spouse. Closely following: job loss and moving. Thanks, Universe. I have to wonder what you could possibly be thinking!

Yesterday, I called my landlord and told him I'm losing my job and will have to move out.

"Of course," he said sadly. Our landlord worked in the same building as Wayne at Sears corporate. Wayne would hand-deliver the rent check to him every month.

"We'll have to start showing it to potential renters soon. Do you mind?" The thought of strangers walking around our home made me sick to my stomach. The idea of random people living here is unfathomable. *Yes, I mind.*

"No, I don't mind," I whispered. "Thanks for understanding."

They'll walk through the front door—the same door that I threw open in a panic when I left work to check on Wayne. They'll tour the living room where we spent most of our time. The kitchen where we practiced our first dance for our wedding and learned how to cook new meals. The dining room where we sat around the table and played games. Hung out with our friends. Discovered new music. Addressed our wedding invitations. The garage that holds his college bins that he never unpacked…our wedding decor. Go up the stairs, and they'll find the backdrop of a video he had of me climbing up on all fours, laughing our asses off because I was too drunk to walk normally. They'll be walking on Goose's favorite area, where she plays fetch with hair ties and tries to push them over the edge to land on the lamp below.

They will look at our framed engagement portraits on the stairwell wall and think to themselves, *Awww. What a nice couple.* They'll have no idea that as the police carried Wayne's body down the stairs, they knocked that photo right off the wall. They'll enter the master bedroom where our canvases from Paint Nite are hung. Where we spent countless hours in bed. Sleeping, talking, laughing, playing. Cuddling with the cats. Talking about our future. They'll continue to the master bathroom where we got ready together. Brushed our teeth next to each other.

And then, they will cross the hallway and walk into the next room. *That* room. The room that displays the Boston shadow box we made together of his favorite memories from his summer internship. The room that holds his framed bachelor's degree diploma from the college we went to. The room that has his video games lined up neatly on the bookcase. The room that holds his clothes—some tucked neatly and clean in his closet; some dirty, draped in his hamper. The room that houses his guitars, both electric and acoustic, and the deer painting he created with me one night. The room where he kept all the notes, cards, books, and gifts I gave him.

The bed. The bed he took his final breaths in. The bed that still has the same sheets, blankets, and pillowcases. The bed that I found him in. The bed that I pulled his body from to the ground. The bed that I wish I would have crawled into and laid on, in his arms for one last time, before calling 911.

Will they feel it? Will they sense it? They'll have no idea of the pain, distress, loneliness, heartbreak, love, and tragedy that happened here. And soon, our stuff will be gone. The home will stand empty until they move their things in, and everything will be different. There will be no evidence that we lived our lives here. Got married here. Died here. Our life together in this home will no longer exist.

JULY 23, 2018

I wonder if I'll ever have another good day. What do I even define as *good*? I've only moved from this bed a couple of times per day over the last few weeks. I really don't even know what to write or think about, but if I don't do something, I'll just disappear.

I don't feel like I exist. I spend most of my time asleep, with infrequent bathroom breaks. I'm not drinking water or eating. I don't remember my last shower, and I haven't brushed my teeth in four days. I'm so thankful for dry shampoo.

I leave my windows open with the air conditioning running, and it feels like I have some sort of connection to the outside world. Plus, at least then I can hear the cicadas. It's cicada season, my very favorite time of year—when the balmy dusks are exploding with the cicadas' song, and the nights are illuminated with fireflies. I love everything about them. Their beautiful buggy eyes. Their fluorescent wings. The shells they leave behind on trees.

I miss our summer night walks spent searching for them. I've done these walks by myself. I've done them with friends and family. But everyone just thinks I'm weird, except for you. You were the only one who understood my love for cicadas. Last year, we saw one on the sidewalk. You picked it up and let it crawl all over you, so I could get a closer look at it. I loved you so much at that moment. I felt so grateful that I was spending my life with someone who just got me.

"Record it!" you screamed, laughing as the prickly legs stuck to your clammy skin.

Now, when I hear the cicadas, I just think back to how happy I was, and how I may never feel that way again. Knowing that I will carry this loss on my shoulders in some shape or form for the rest of my life is unfathomable. It destroys any hope I may have once had and leaves me frozen in fear. Everything I once loved is tainted with impossible memories.

I'm moving out tomorrow. My family helped box up the house, and our friends are coming over to help me move. We moved into this place alone during the middle of the night a few years ago. We used my parents' van and made more than fifteen trips back and forth—just the two of us, lifting and cramming in every piece of old furniture and hand-me-down we owned.

Exhausted, we collapsed on our old queen-size mattress on the floor—the mattress you would die on not even two years later—at 5 a.m. surrounded by McDonald's bags and breakfast burritos. It was a simple life, but one we loved. It was all we needed.

JULY 30, 2018

Time has flown by since my decision to try life on the road. The months have felt like weeks, and after packing up our entire lives and leaving everything I knew behind, everything unfolded at once.

"What will you do on this trip? How long will you be gone?" our friend Shaun asked one night in a drunken haze of grief. We had met Shaun in college and stayed in touch into adulthood, and he quickly became one of our closest friends.

"Whatever I want," I replied. "I'm just going to go where the wind takes me. Nothing's planned. I just want to be alone in nature with no expectations, no responsibility, no materialistic things. I just wanna exist in peace with Wayne's ashes."

Shaun has been helpful ever since Wayne died, as he conveniently lives only about twenty minutes from me in an apartment with his parents. He has spent the last few months coming over after his shifts, cleaning my place and taking care of things around the house that I'd deemed unimportant to my survival. He picks up burritos from the Mexican restaurant around the corner for dinner, forces me outside for walks, helps take care of the cats, and talks about Wayne whenever I want.

Mostly, though, I think we're both just lonely. We spend a lot of long nights on the couch with the cats, zoning out to *Full House* and *Roseanne* reruns while I pretend this isn't my life.

The arrangement works, for now. Spending time with him feels like I have a tiny piece of Wayne with me somehow. With their similar interests in food, travel, and more, he has made it easier to honor Wayne's lifestyle. He's encouraged me when I'm too depressed to shower and taken care of things that I didn't even know I needed to have done.

I came home from work one day and found he'd cleaned out my closet while I was gone, something I'd been silently avoiding for months. A stack of clean, folded laundry sat at the foot of my bed, complete with my underwear and bras. I was immediately embarrassed, but the embarrassment was soon replaced by curiosity. *Who would do something like this? Should I be creeped out or thankful?* My eyes narrowed in on a gray sheet draped delicately over my sparkling wedding dress, not looked at or touched since the wedding. *How did he know things I only thought about in the darkest parts of my mind?*

I'd hated seeing that dress in the closet, but I'd had no mental or physical energy to do anything about it. What was I going to do with it anyway? It was three hundred dollars, on clearance at David's Bridal, and not something I felt compelled to keep, but I was terrified of any other options.

"How did you know?" I asked. I'd never said anything to anyone about my dress hanging sadly in the corner of my closet.

"I just didn't think I'd want to look at it if I were you."

He also cleaned out my pantry, throwing out old, expired food and empty jars of peanut butter I left on the shelves. He's made a lot of Korean dishes from his mom's recipes and made sure the fridge was stocked. He always makes sure the litter box is scooped, and he helps me give Goose her allergy medicine.

I'm so grateful for the help, and I've thanked Wayne for bringing someone so empathetic into my life. Shaun and I both benefit from our friendship. He gets to escape from his parents' house and smoke all the weed he wants, freely displaying his tattoos, including the one we got together with a group of friends as a memorial for Wayne. He can act more like himself when he isn't around his strict parents. And his presence soothes me in a way I wasn't sure anyone else could. He's soft-spoken but assertive, something I admire.

"What if I quit my job and came with you? At least, for part of it?" His question brought me back to reality. "I'll do it right now." He grabbed his phone, looking at me expectantly.

So many conflicting thoughts raced through my head. It would be nice to have someone around, but I really wanted to do this alone. That was the original point: to learn how to be by myself, forever. To show that I can do this without anyone's help. To grieve in peace. If Shaun came with, all of that would disappear. He knew how important this was to me. I couldn't help but to feel imposed on and pressured in the moment, although it wasn't a terribly bad idea.

"I have ten thousand dollars saved," he offered, filling the silence that my long pause created. "You wouldn't be paying my way."

I'm sure my parents would feel better about it. Everyone is convinced I'm not going to come back. To be fair, I'm not convinced either. Maybe having someone in the passenger seat would hold me accountable. Maybe I'd accomplish more.

I've already packed my stuff, and I'll be living out of a couple of duffel bags. I've got nothing else to lose. Nothing to prove to anyone. Besides, nothing is permanent. *What could go wrong?*

"Why not? Be ready in a few days."

ii. the spiral

"Come to the woods, for here is rest."
—John Muir, 1916

i sat alone
behind the wall i built
to protect my heart
my mind, my soul
tears frozen to cheeks
like melting icicles
dripping
fading
changing
spiraling
welcome to rock bottom,
how long will you be staying?

AUGUST 3, 2018

Badlands National Park, South Dakota

I rolled up my musty sleeping bag and wet clothes and packed away the damp tent. It was bright, brilliant, and dry outside, with no signs of the surprise storm that had suddenly attacked us during the night. Dark blue skies collided with the sandy beige earth. The day was hot, and insects were already screaming in the background. The other well-rested campers near us were drying out their rainflies and already had breakfast underway.

"We slept too long," Shaun said, nodding in the direction of their sites. "Let's just go." We decided our gear could wait to dry out until we got to our next stop. I wasn't planning on spending extensive time in the Badlands, since I knew the area well. We fit everything back into the overflowing car and drove to the first trailhead.

This was my fourth time exploring the desolate land. My grandparents took me and my sister as small children on a road trip in their van in the early nineties, and my parents took us again on our way to Yellowstone and the Grand Tetons years later. I loved visiting the tiny old tourist town of Wall Drug, being confused at the Corn Palace, and driving through the

Black Hills—hitting Mount Rushmore, Crazy Horse Memorial, and Custer State Park along the way. Memories of my now-dead grandparents surfaced as I thought back to my love for road trips and exploring nature.

"Bad, bad, bad, bad, bad LANDS!" my grandpa had screamed into the vast, empty wilderness as I hid behind him, scared to get too close to the edge of the massive craters in the earth. His shouts echoed through the canyons and bounced off the walls into the prairieland. He picked me up and held me high, so I could feel what he felt. I clutched onto the pale-yellow rubber snake he bought me at the gift shop the day before as I peered out from behind his shoulder.

Green grasses and wildflowers blanketed the park's 243 thousand acres, disrupted by colorful towering buttes, pinnacles, and spires. This dramatic landscape houses bison, bighorn sheep, and prairie dogs. It has one of the world's richest fossil beds with horse, rhino, and saber-toothed cat remains.

I'd taken Wayne on this same road trip to recreate the magic I'd discovered with my family all those years ago. Flashbacks of Wayne rolling down his window and making ridiculous sounds at the bison filled my mind as we drove down the dusty open road.

A small smile formed across my lips, as these memories seemed so fresh. Just five years ago, we were in this same place. I wondered how things could look exactly the same while my life was so heartbreakingly different.

Shaun and I arrived at the start of the trailhead, and I hiked out into the open-but-maze-like terrain, taking twists and turns without necessarily paying attention to my route, leaving Shaun to take his own path. The pinnacles around me were striped with reds, whites, pinks, and yellows—jagged edges jutting into the sky like a scene from Mars. I walked and walked, carefully following the rock cairns stacked together to ensure I knew how to get back.

The scene was so expansively flat and interestingly chaotic all at once, a cross between a dull, dry desert and a luscious prairie with vibrant grasses and roaming wildlife. I sat down on the butte—dangling my legs over the edge—as I looked out over the expansive land and breathed in the arid air. *This is what it means to feel free.*

After a few more hours exploring, we relocated to the next campground for the night. We took an evening drive down a scenic road before hiking to Hay Butte Overlook, an eroded, rugged wasteland of peaks and valleys.

I reached into the glovebox and pulled out the cardboard scatter tube, adorned with some religious quote about death on a label on the side. I had brought enough of Wayne's ashes for each national park and left the rest at home. I tucked the tube into my pack, and Shaun and I started to walk. This is where I wanted to spread the first portion during my time on the road.

The air was heavy with buzzing beetles and clicking grasshoppers, but the silence still cut through the ambient noise. The setting sun cast a pale-pink glow on the sand-colored buttes.

The land was dotted with hundreds of holes and tunnels, home to the cute but elusive prairie dogs. As we walked by, they chirped, running into their shelters and peeking their tiny heads out before slowly guarding their entrance on a mound of dirt, alerting the rest of their town to danger if needed.

Wayne had loved the prairie dogs on our trip to the Badlands. I know he wanted to take one home, just like he did with every other animal we encountered.

This was the perfect place. I grabbed the scattering tube, wishing I had an easier way to transport it. The lid wasn't flush, so white dust coated the inside of my backpack. I winced. Wayne's ashes were the most important thing I had with me, and I couldn't even keep him safe. Once again, I felt guilty, like a failure and a bad wife. I opened the container slowly, and a white cloud filled the dry air. Plenty.

I gently shook a teaspoon-sized amount into the container's cap and handed Shaun my phone.

"I feel like I should document it each time," I told him. "Can you take a short video of the scatter at every park?"

"Yeah, good idea."

I positioned myself away from the wind.

"OK, go," he said.

"Uhh…it's August third? Fourth? Here at Badlands National Park at Hay Butte Overlook. I'm gonna, uhh, spread Wayne's ashes here."

I turned from Shaun and the camera and looked out in front of me, tears forming in the corners of my eyes.

"A little to your left," he whispered softly.

I sighed and dumped the capful of ashes into the wind. Instead of being taken off the cliff by the gusts and dispersed through the valley, the ashes blew back into my face and neck. I looked back at the camera, embarrassed.

"Guess it's a good thing I'll be getting lots of practice."

On the way back to the campground, a group of horses blocked the road, roaming free under the setting sun. They walked up to the stopped car and started to bite my windshield wipers, acting as interested in us as we were in them.

Back at our site, I popped the back hatch of my small, dark-gray Nissan and pulled out a tiny, hard-sided cooler full of spices, seasonings, sauce packets of all different kinds, and a couple of cans of Beefaroni. We weren't keeping a lot of fresh food around, but we had a few baskets of canned goods and some freeze-dried meals, peanut butter, crackers, soups, trail mix, beef jerky, dried fruit, cashews, and other non-perishable things that were easy to heat up over a fire or in a cast-iron pan on a small stove with a can of propane.

An overflowing Ziploc bag full of clear pill pockets fell out of the cooler. They were full of ground psilocybin, something Shaun brought along to help cope with the depression and constant dissociation.

"Hey, wanna?" I held up the bag.

"I thought we were saving them for long hikes and rainy days," he said.

I made a face. Grief doesn't wait for long hikes and rainy days.

"Remember what happened last time?" he said, almost father-like.

I did remember. My face grew hot with shame and guilt.

It had been a particularly lonely night, not long before leaving for the road. I bought mushrooms from my massage therapist after learning how they can rewire your brain and help encourage positive thinking. Shaun and I tried them a few times on camping trips, and I felt amazing while hiking through the brown murky rivers and prairielands of Illinois. I met wildfire-burnt trees and talked with them about their pasts. I laid on the soft grass and watched bright white clouds roll by and neon green leaves flutter in the wind, and I understood what they were trying to communicate to me.

But that night had been different. It was nighttime, and I was inside all day, contemplating things I'd never once thought I was capable of. Shaun came over after a long shift, and I'd felt instant relief as we smashed a few smelly mushroom tops and stems together in between a peanut butter and jelly sandwich. Not too long after, I felt needy and touch-deprived. I was physically starved. We were in my bed watching *Planet Earth* like we'd done on so many days in the past. I brought my fingertips up to his back and started drawing circles on his smooth, tan skin. Suddenly, it felt like I hadn't touched anyone in years. The warmth of his skin radiated through mine as I gently ran my nails up and down the length of his torso, followed by a trail of goosebumps. I stopped, but things escalated, and after that night, things were never quite the same. I felt incredibly guilty and heartbroken, having erased Wayne as my last sexual experience. It didn't mean anything, we decided. No kissing, no emotion. Just friends with benefits. Something to distract me from my hellish life and to pass the time. Something to help me feel real, like I actually existed on the same plane as everyone else.

Trying to shake the memory, I sighed and closed the hatch. After gathering some wood from the surrounding area, I grabbed my dull hatchet, a lighter, and a tuft of dryer lint from the fire-starter bag. I stripped some small shavings of wood from the logs with my hatchet, creating enough for kindling. I opened the cans of Beefaroni with a can opener and set them aside.

It was hot and dry, so the fire started quickly and easily. Soon it was roaring, the flames way too high to heat the cans directly.

"What are you doing?" Shaun asked, coming up from behind me.

"Making dinner," I answered.

"That flame is way too high for that." He grabbed the cans from the picnic table. "Don't do it like that."

"I know," I said. "I was waiting for the fire to calm down before I did anything." *Why did I feel the need to explain myself? I've been camping my entire life. I can do something as simple as heat up a can of Chef Boyardee.*

Or can I?

He constructed some kind of complicated stand with aluminum foil to hold the cans and heated them up himself. I'd planned to just let the flame die, put the cans on the wood stack I made, and be done with it, but I was happy to let him take over if he had a better way.

We ate from the cans with metal sporks, and I grabbed my canvas bag of books. I brought so many widow and grief books with me—*Second Firsts, Widow to Widow, Option B, A Grief Observed.* But after browsing through the titles, I decided I didn't want to read about anyone else's grief. I had enough of my own.

In the beginning, all I could do was obsess over other young widows. *Who else felt like me? Was anyone else this sad? Please, there must be someone who understands.* I consumed every new blog or internet post and support group available. Despite the yearn for connection and a community that understood me, I had trouble reading or comprehending anything these days. I could read the same paragraph twenty times and not realize I had read anything at all. I could read bullet point after bullet point but be unable to rehash anything my eyes and brain touched. I was fried.

I spent the rest of the evening lying on the hard picnic table, looking up at the stars, wishing there were trees around to hang the hammock from.

I climbed, tear-stricken, into the tent—a routine so familiar it felt wrong when I didn't cry myself to sleep or accumulate a layer of salt under my eyes. Seconds later, I heard a howl in the distance. Followed by another. And another. More and more chimed in, until what seemed like hundreds of coyotes were harmonizing to their own sad song of the night. Their sound was comforting in a tragic way, and I fell asleep to their wild lullaby.

AUGUST 5, 2018

We left the Badlands and began the quick drive to Wind Cave National Park after sampling some homemade shrimp and grits from the camp store kitchen. While exiting the park gates, we got stuck behind the fumes of hundreds of motorcycles gathering in the area for Sturgis, the largest motorcycle rally in the world. Sturgis started in 1938, and the ten-day adventure has grown to welcome over 500,000 riders over the years. It felt like all 500,000 were in front of us for the entire hour drive to Wind Cave.

Wind Cave National Park is known for its vast, underground wind cave, one of the longest and most complex cave systems in the world. The cave's walls have honeycomb-shaped calcite formations called boxwork that we got to see during the underground guided tour. Being underground in the dark and chilly silence took me out of my head and demanded my presence.

My eyes slowly adjusted to the dark, and I could hear water dripping from the cave ceiling to the damp floor. We wound our way through different rooms while cowering at cave crickets and learning about the different rock formations. At the end, the heavy door opened back up into the bright world, exposing the endless prairie and pine forests that are home to bison, elk, and pronghorn antelope.

Back above ground, my stress came back. I'd declined a hike earlier that morning in the Badlands that I thought would be too hard for me. It was hot, and I was out of shape.

Both Wayne and I had struggled with our fitness on and off throughout our relationship. During college and after, we both gained a considerable amount of weight, landing me at the heaviest I'd ever been on October 15, 2016—the day he proposed.

After he died, I'd stopped eating for a short time. Not only did food remind me of all that I'd lost, but I also had no desire for the things I'd once loved. I had no appetite. It got to the point where I would just eat a couple of spoonfuls of peanut butter before bed, and that was it for the day.

I'd had no confidence in myself to make it up that first steep switchback on the trail back at the Badlands. I still wasn't eating much, and I wasn't up for the challenge. I just wanted to lie in the tent listening to the grunts of the nearby elk and feel sorry for myself, so that's what I did. I didn't get the opportunity to take that decision back. I later regretted it, but there was nothing I could do once it was done.

"It was my favorite hike from the trip so far," Shaun said. "You should have come. It wasn't even that hard."

After getting back to camp, I took a hit and felt that familiar high take over.

I used to be so against weed, growing up in the D.A.R.E (Drug Abuse Resistance Education) era of the nineties, where police stood in front of an elementary school classroom and threatened us with saying no to drugs. D.A.R.E. eventually lost funding and failed in 1998. A study done by the University of Illinois stated the program was counterproductive, and the students who participated were more likely to use drugs, not less.

There came a point early in my grieving process, however, where it was just too painful to continue without help. I didn't have health insurance. When I realized marijuana could help with my anxiety and depression and eliminate recurring nightmares, I was grateful for an opportunity to self-medicate. It was the only thing that helped me sleep, eat, and settle my mind. Not only did it put me in a better mood, but it also helped me appreciate things that my sober mind no longer appreciated—which was pretty much everything. It gave me an escape. It took me out of reality and surrounded me in a more comforting fog than grief-brain.

At this point, the only time I wasn't high was when I was asleep.

I fell asleep under the stars, thinking about my goals and what I wanted to accomplish on this trip: Improve my mental and physical health. Work on my spirituality. Practice self-care. Grieve, grieve, grieve. Survive on the basics, without the comforts of home. Feel small within the universe and among the circle of life. Find my purpose. Search for an answer—any answer. Anything that would help guide me down the right path. Anything that would help me survive.

After taking several days to explore Mount Rushmore, the Black Hills, and Theodore Roosevelt National Park in North Dakota, we arrived in Yellowstone National Park via Beartooth Highway.

Beartooth Highway had been one of Wayne's favorite drives on a past road trip, and I was terrified of doing it again. I didn't know how I'd react to being there without him.

It felt surreal, making the same twists and turns we'd made all those years ago. Stopping at the same overlooks. Taking in the same scenery. I felt him with me all day; his presence was strong. I wondered if he could feel the anguish I was feeling. I hoped he couldn't. I was almost jealous that he wasn't here to also go through this agony. And then I felt guilty for feeling that way.

"Let's pull off and hike down a little bit," I urged Shaun as I got out of the car.

I walked across the guardrail-less road and onto the other side of the mountain. I scooted carefully down a steep cliff, with a goal of getting a better view of the sapphire-blue lake down in a valley of glaciers surrounded by snowcapped peaks. Brilliantly colored flowers painted the mountainside with bright purples, pinks, yellows, blues, and whites. A family of pure-white mountain goats crossed over a snowy ravine, not too far from where I stood. Their hooves glided over the slick ice and snow, but they weren't scared of falling.

I felt so serene and alone on my own magical mountain—full of fake fairytale surprises, only it was very real. I scattered some of Wayne's ashes through the snow after the goats disappeared, and I imagined the wind carrying some down and into one of the crystal blue lakes that dotted the valley below.

AUGUST 18, 2018

As the days went by, I got more comfortable with our routine. I was getting high all day every day and hiking non-stop. I floated around in a grief and THC-induced fog, questioning what I was doing on Earth, who I was, and why any of this mattered. We ate ramen noodles, canned soup, and freeze-dried meals using a small, electric kettle. We used one cast-iron pan for any dish we made that was more elaborate, so all we had to do was rinse it out at a potable water spigot and pat it dry until we pulled it out from under the passenger seat for another meal.

After a few rest days in our first campsite, we were ready for more adventure. We packed our bags and headed for Fairy Falls Trail, a five-mile hike near Grand Prismatic Spring, the largest hot spring in the US and the third largest in the world. Grand Prismatic Spring has been written about in literature countless times, even as far back as 1871, and there's no wonder why. Bigger than a football field, the commanding spring demands everyone's respect. Bright orange, yellow, and green bands border the deep, sapphire middle, resembling a rainbow eye from a different universe. It's impossible to understand the sheer size and depth of the magical geothermal pool, even when standing on the boardwalk above. The heat, residual steam, and rotten eggs permeated the air and my clothes, totally immersing my senses. A new energy ran through me, connecting and grounding my body. I'd stood in this exact spot twice before— once as a child with my parents and older sister, and once with Wayne.

This time, it was different. I was different. My new grief added a complex layer of emotion, reminding me that this spring was here long before me, and would be here long after. After so many years, it was exactly how I had left it, but I was so different. So small, so insignificant, so fleeting. Just another speck on this planet who would live and die and leave nothing behind to show for it. I closed my eyes and pictured myself diving inside from the boardwalk, pushing deeper and deeper into the dark blue water, leaving it all behind. Suddenly everything felt lighter, less serious. The weight of the world melted off my shoulders; the warmth radiated through my skin and engulfed me.

We slowly left the spring behind and continued into the forest behind the active ground. A few miles into the hike— after passing a tall, wispy waterfall, a field of half-burnt tree trunks, and bright orange, boiling creeks that ran into cold-water streams—I saw something move out of the corner of my eye. During my silent gaze, I realized I was staring at a wild porcupine as he made his rounds without a care in the world, against a stunning backdrop of towering mountains. I wondered if I could stay in that moment forever. I felt a calming peace wash over me as I observed the silent creature.

I gave him a big head start and then followed him down the canopied trail, out into a small clearing amidst the trees. The ground here was different. Buzzing. Alive. Steam rose from a large crater in the center of the clearing, surrounded by bubbling mud pots and cracked dirt piles. The ground transformed from a buzz to a slight vibration before a rush of water came crashing through the crater, spouting high into the air before it bubbled back down again.

"Did you see that?!" I asked both Shaun and the porcupine, which didn't seem to notice anything different. The spiky creature disappeared into the forest soon after, and Shaun and I returned to our route down the trail, blood pumping and hearts beating from adrenaline. We didn't see another person for the entire five miles, and I was at peace.

I saw a movement to the right by some dead trees and willow patches. I stopped, waiting to see if something would emerge. The warm breeze rustled through the canopy, causing the spruce trees to creak and groan. Suddenly, a tiny, cute little thing with light-brown and white fur peeked out of his hiding spot and came out into the filtered sun rays.

"Look at this cute little guy," Shaun exclaimed with a high-pitched giggle. "Seymour."

"He absolutely looks like a Seymour," I agreed.

Seymour climbed out from in between the bleached, dead trees and onto his hind legs. He was so tiny, he almost looked like a baby. He sniffed the air and inched a little closer, and a little closer, until he was within arm's reach. We stood completely still, our eyes darting between Seymour's and each other's, not moving a muscle for fear of scaring him back into hiding. We were all trusting each other in that moment, until a bird took off from a branch, and he was gone, his tiny body finding his way back home. We'd later find out he was a short-tailed weasel, and I would think of him often.

I was looking down at my feet at the roots and rocks while we walked in silence. About a mile from civilization, I heard a faint, low, grunt that stopped me in my tracks. I slowly raised my head to meet whatever it was face-to-face. *Bear? Cougar?* I didn't know what I'd rather face if I had a choice. But no, we had hiked right into a herd of angry female elk protecting their young, which may have been worse. The grunty girl started to walk toward us, slowly but confidently following the trail. A few other elk took notice and started to back her up, like a gang, creating a protective barrier around their offspring.

"Holy shit," I whispered, trying not to move my mouth too much. "What do we do?" My instincts told me to back up slowly, but I had no way of knowing if this was the right approach. I did it anyway.

"Back up," I whispered louder. There was a tree to the right of us, just slightly off the trail. If we could just get behind it, we'd at least have something in between us. We had bear spray back at camp, but what good would that do us now? I started to shuffle my feet sideways while moving slowly, careful not to turn my back on the animal. The precepted safety of the tree felt so close but so far. But why hadn't Shaun moved?

"Cyn, let's just move to the side and keep going." Red flags went off and my gut said no way, but I immediately second-guessed my ability to listen to what my body told me to do. *But what if he's right? He always seems to be.* This wasn't the time or place to disagree, but I did not want to walk through a herd of female elk who were clearly warning us to keep away.

With that, I quickly ducked behind the tree, leaving Shaun out on the trail with the largest female, who was still moving toward him.

"Shaun, why? Come on."

He was going to get himself seriously hurt, or worse. I hid behind the trunk, trying to convince him this was the better way. Finally, he stepped off the trail and behind the tree next to me.

"Well, what's your plan now?" he turned to face me. The elk had stopped pursuing but was still standing strong and knew we were behind the tree.

"I don't know!" I said, exasperated. "But at least this buys us a few more seconds to think things through. And maybe now we're not a threat!"

I slid down the length of the trunk to a crouch to catch my breath. I peeked around the side and saw the leader had walked back to the rest of the herd, but they were still on edge and guarding the trail.

"Phweeeee!" *Clap clap clap.* A shrill, high-pitched whistle pierced through the forest. "Phweee!" *Clap clap clap.*

I turned my head sharply toward the sound and saw a young woman around the same age as me with a long brown braid, shorts, a tank top, and a bright green backpack. She barreled down the trail the opposite way from our route.

"Git! Git on, now!"

The herd disbanded. Some of them ran toward our tree, ignoring us as they raced down the ravine. The others ran up the opposite way, clearing a path for the human warrior. I watched in awe as the woman hiked confidently through the parted elk, spotting us on her way.

"You just haveta sneak up on 'em first," she yelled back, smiling, but not slowing her pace. "You gotta scare 'em before they scare you."

We stayed in Yellowstone for fourteen days—exploring the towering waterfalls, geothermal attractions, colorful canyons, expansive lakes, sprawling meadows, boiling rivers, and near-vertical hikes with expansive mountain and forest vistas. We tackled every section of the park and stayed in different campgrounds depending on location.

We had cut it close when we had to line up for a spot before

6 a.m. one morning, with no guarantee of a place to sleep. We waited and waited with sixteen other hopefuls; surely enough people were leaving on a Sunday, and we could all secure a site.

The early morning air was frigid, and our breath was visible, even in mid-August, as we all exchanged travel stories and favorite tips about Yellowstone. My eyes darted from car to car. They were doing one of two things: checking out or leaving to explore for the day. I'd started to get nervous around 10:30 when the stream of cars to check out wasn't as long as the line of humans in front of us. We had been waiting for over four hours at that point and were planning on staying at this campground for several days. The line in front of us slowly got shorter, until there was only one group left between us and a spot. They left happily, and I sat on the curb, fiddling with my shoelace. There were still a handful of groups behind us, but it was already after 11 a.m. I wasn't hopeful, but the park ranger assigning the campsites told us people leave late all the time. We still had a chance.

Finally, at 11:30, the ranger came back outside.

"You made it," he said. "You're the last site of the day. Sorry folks! Come back tomorrow!" he shouted down the line at the others.

Shaun and I jumped up from the curb, and he gathered me up into a tight embrace. "Damn," he smiled bigger than I'd ever seen. "I did not think we were going to get this lucky."

From then on, we were awake first thing in the morning and out until almost midnight. It stayed light until late, and we stopped at Lamar Valley each evening to search for animals. The river valley was home to herds of elk, bison, grizzlies, and wolf packs. We'd sit in the car and share a joint with the windows down—listening to the distant grunts of bison while exchanging memories of Wayne and watching the sun dip behind the rolling mountains and deep valleys—until dusk faded into twilight. The stars would appear almost instantly, shimmering between the occasional meteor on the horizon, lighting up the night sky as we dreamed about the trip ahead. The long days both dragged on and flew by in a warm haze of summer wildflowers and dusty sunsets. Over the two weeks we spent in Yellowstone, we watched bison walk through campgrounds, rest beside tents, and piss on parking lots. I fell asleep to coyotes most nights, hooting owls on the others. We spent an entire day snuggled in our sleeping bags inside the tent during a violent thunderstorm, until the next day came, and the rain was gone. We watched coyotes hunt and catch a marmot and listened as the helpless marmot family cried in its wake while the coyote carried the limp, swinging, brown body back to its den. We made breakfasts with what we could find at camp stores and did laundry and dishes under water spigots coming from the ground.

I wanted more. I had the crazy idea to go to Alaska, which wasn't in my original plan, and we spent an entire day at a visitor center with crappy cell service, booking tickets from Seattle in September. We'd only been on the road for a little over two weeks, but life kept going—even though I was stuck in the past.

AUGUST 26, 2018

Grand Teton National Park, Wyoming

We headed to the Tetons for a few days with a plan to spend another week in Yellowstone after that, since we couldn't stay there for more than fourteen consecutive days (which we'd already maxed out). We decided to hit the west side of the Tetons area first.

To take advantage of the park in a short amount of time, we did a long, eight-mile hike around Jenny Lake, amidst one of the most beautiful mountain scenes I could dream of. We shared the trail with several other groups and even a black bear, but he had no interest in us as he munched on foliage and roots.

I wanted to go rafting in the Grand Canyon, but I wasn't due to visit Arizona until the winter, so we stayed near the Snake River in the Tetons and jumped on an early morning raft tour.

Floating down the river, the guide let me sit up on top of the raft, front and center. I think she could tell I was here for something more. As we bobbed along the fast-moving areas, I felt alone in the wilderness, with nothing in front of me but ice-cold rapids, trees, and cliffsides. A bald eagle soared overhead, and two deer were in the forest to the left. We arrived at a calm area, and the guide told me to stand on the side and top of the raft. She started spinning us in circles until I flew off, clothes on and unprepared, into the icy but inviting water. I resurfaced and looked up, slightly shaken but filled with adrenaline. As I held onto my life vest and floated on my back, looking up at the blue morning sky, I felt weightless. A minute and large splash later, Shaun was next to me. We doggy-paddled next to the raft together while she talked about the different wildlife in the area.

I reached over the side of the raft, opened my waterproof pack, grabbed the bottle with Wayne's ashes, and let some go in the river next to me. He sparkled like tiny diamonds, swirling with the current.

Sirens. In the rearview mirror and in my ears.

Panic. In my throat and in my soul.

"Do something!" Shaun said, gesturing to the bottle of Febreze. But I was frozen. It was too late anyway. We were already pulling over to the side of the road. I was still coughing from my last hit.

The cop walked over to my window while I fumbled with the bowl and lighter, trying to hide it while acting normal—not something I was so great at after getting high.

"Do you know why I pulled y'all over?" he asked, complete with a cowboy-type hat and prying eyes.

"I was going ten over, but just following traffic," Shaun piped up from the driver's seat. "We're going back to Yellowstone for a week until we leave for Montana."

The officer collected our information and started returning to his car.

I let out a huge sigh. Maybe he didn't smell it. He definitely would have said something. I picked at my dirty fingernails and watched him walk back to his vehicle through the mirror. My palms were sweaty and waves of fear mixed with indifference took over my body.

"What should we do?" I said out of the side of my mouth, careful not to move my head or any other part of my body. I didn't want to make any sudden movements or seem suspicious.

"I can't believe you didn't get the spray," he answered, disapproval in his voice. The cop came back up to my side of the car.

"How much marijuana do y'all have in the vehicle?"

I glanced over at Shaun, unable to answer for myself. "Well…whatever is in this grinder," he said, handing it over. The cop took it and left again.

I had a million thoughts running through my head, but when you're already at rock bottom, you don't care about things to the extent that a normal person would.

Shaun had lied.

We had several ounces of weed to last us months on the road, with many different pieces of paraphernalia. And our mushroom pills were right in the back.

The *before* me would have felt my throat in my stomach. I would have panicked, imagining all the ways my life was going to be ruined. The *new* me just sat there with my skull pressed into the headrest, watching my breath fog up the window I'd rolled up, hoping the officer would go to the other side next time.

He did.

"There's nothing here." He showed us our pitiful evidence.

"Here, take this." Shaun handed over his black fanny pack full of weed.

The cop glanced inside and asked if we were sure this was all we had.

"Yep."

He went back to his car again. I wondered if he was going to take it and smoke it himself or really get us busted.

"Why do you keep lying to him?!" I hissed. "It's going to be easier if we just cooperate." He dismissed me.

Eventually the cop walked up to my car one last time, letting us know he must search everything and was waiting for backup.

I'm out in the middle of nowhere, getting busted for drugs while high out of my mind, and now cops will be taking every last tampon out of my car. What is my life?

They instructed us to sit on the dead, downed, and hollow log in the nearby ditch. I sat there tearing grass out of the earth, blade by blade, watching my only possessions being thrown about and discarded like trash. *Who am I?*

"What are these? Bath salts?" The cop's words took me out of my trance. I looked up from my green distraction and saw Wayne's ashes in his hand.

"Wait!" I screamed, trying to prevent him from spilling any or throwing them in the ditch.

"That's her dead husband," Shaun shouted.

Dumbfounded, the cop asked me to explain. I told him everything. About how I'd married the love of my life, and that he'd died six weeks later. How I found his body hours after his heart stopped, and I couldn't save him. How I lost myself that day too, and that I was just trying to keep my promises by staying alive and taking him with me.

The cop pulled me aside. "How well do you know him?" he asked me curiously, gesturing to Shaun.

"I mean...I've known him for like eight years," I said apprehensively. "Why?"

"We found a scale in his backpack, and we think he might be meeting his friends across the country to sell these drugs," he said with a completely straight face. He held up the mushroom pills, pipes, and lighters.

I didn't know what was more comical, the thought that Shaun had friends across the entire country that he was distributing a bunch of cheap weed and mushroom pills to, or the fact that they thought a few ounces was too much for us to smoke over a few months.

"No," I said forcefully, trying to hold back my amusement. "I'm only here to connect with nature, get away from people, hike, and find a new purpose. I just need to feel alive. He's only along for the ride." I stole a glance at Shaun behind me with the other cop. I hoped he was giving him the same story.

The cop speaking with me went back to his partner, and they gave us both sobriety tests in the middle of the Wyoming wilderness.

Families in minivans on vacation rolled down their windows as they drove by, braking and gawking with their kids' heads sticking out with wide eyes and tongues to match their dogs. I followed the officer's pen with my eyes and walked a straight line down the cracked mountain road.

I thought about the bison causing roadblocks from people who were gawking and taking pictures, and I promised myself I would never gawk at these animals again. Being the subject of the gawking didn't feel good.

"Well, you have a choice," the cop said, after I somehow passed my sobriety test. "One of you can go to jail, or both of you can go."

What? One of us or both of us? Do they feel bad for me? Are they giving me an out?

"You're free to go if he comes with us," the cop added, nodding Shaun's way. Again, I felt frozen. I didn't know what to say or how to react. It *was* his weed—that I paid half for. He was the one driving and speeding at the time, and the reason we got pulled over in the first place.

He called Shaun over and gave him the same ultimatum. "I'll go," he said immediately.

My eyes widened, and I felt an instant rush of guilt engulf my body. *We wouldn't be here if it weren't for me*, I told myself. If Wayne hadn't died and I wasn't such a mess. If I went alone like I wanted to. None of this would be happening.

They turned him around and cuffed him. I watched helplessly as they guided him into the back of the police car, our stuff scattered on the side of the road. I started gathering everything up and only half listened as the cop told me I could check in at the station in the morning.

They pulled away one by one, leaving me on the side of road alone. I stood there for a while, listening to the grasshoppers crackle in the tall grass and the distant sound of traffic on the nearby highway. I stuffed our once-organized gear wherever it would fit. After I packed everything away, I got into the driver's seat, barely able to hold in my tears before my body became absorbed by the safety of the gray and black leather that had become my home.

I laid my head on the steering wheel, blinded by the familiar feeling of being alone. I had no cell service and nobody to talk to. I'd finally gotten what I wanted originally on this trip…and I was miserable.

My eyes drifted to the dashboard where I spotted one lighter, one glass bowl, and one side of a silver grinder that had some weed left. *No way.*

I smiled through my shock and tears and started driving back toward the police station, taking a campground recommendation by one of the officers. Not knowing my next steps or anything about the future, I pitched my tent next to two men.

"Hey, where's your man?" the older guy asked, standing up and watching me set up by myself.

"One is dead and one is in jail," I replied with a straight face. I made eye contact with them as I zipped up the see-through nylon barrier between me and everything else, situating the rusty hatchet my parents gave me near my pillow.

It was almost laughable, hearing that sentence out loud. But it was true. I tried to will myself to sleep as I thought of all the different ways this could end. I knew there was no use to stressing over something I couldn't change, but I couldn't believe this is how my trip was going to end after only three weeks. *Am I not supposed to continue? Is there a reason why things got derailed so early on? Was this a sign? Am I meant to be completely alone?*

AUGUST 27, 2018

Teton County Jail

My eyes opened with the early morning light and cold damp chill that crept up the side of my sleeping bag. The hatchet was in the same spot I left it. Immediately, the events from the previous day replayed in my mind while I pulled on my hiking shoes and tightened the laces.

Tiny condensation droplets fell onto my dirty, tangled hair as I unzipped the tent. After using a pit toilet that probably hadn't been cleaned in months, I unclipped the tent fasteners and slid the metal and fiberglass rods out from the loops, disassembling my home in under thirty seconds. I started my car and left before the two curious men in their tent even woke up.

The drive to the jail was silent and somber. The early morning mist was cold, and the grass was wet with dew. My chest was filled with anxiety, knowing I would continue this trip no matter what happened, but I felt overcome with guilt at the thought of leaving my camping companion behind.

My life had transformed into something foreign to me. I had no plan, no set destination, and no timeline. There was no responsibility, no routine, and no real goal other than isolation and grieving.

I'd started babysitting young, working in the mall at fifteen, and always had a job since, working part-time night shifts from midnight to 4 a.m. and writing for both the newspaper and yearbook while going to college full time. For the months I dragged myself into work after Wayne died, my brain just couldn't process anything I didn't care about. I knew I was in no position to find another job, and I didn't want to work anyway.

I wanted to live.

Suddenly, I saw something big out of my left window, which cut off thoughts of my past life.

Moose!

Two dark moose, a mother and a calf, were standing in the middle of a lake on the side of the abandoned road. I pulled over to the side and got out of my car. We'd been talking about seeing moose this whole time, thinking maybe it wouldn't happen until we were further north.

I stared at the duo, their giant heads and muscular bodies lit up by the morning sun. Fog was surrounding them, rising from the cold water they drank. I heard rustling to the left, and a lighter-colored, smaller calf joined them.

I went back to my car and grabbed a flannel blanket from the back. Wrapping the warmth around me, I hopped onto the hood of my car and watched their grand movements, gracefully gliding against the glass-like lake.

My anxiety melted away and I was instantly calmed, knowing that whatever would happen on this day, I'd already experienced my worst nightmare. *I'll get through it*, I knew. I'd just have to keep going.

I didn't want to leave the moose. I felt connected to them in that moment. Just me and them, together in an empty, lonely world. After taking a few pictures for Shaun, I got back into the car and finished my drive to jail. It was time to face reality.

I was parked on the curb for a few hours before deciding to call the station to get an update. "They won't tell us anything," the lady on the phone told me. "Call back later." I hung up—annoyed, nervous, and scared that things might not be going as well as I'd hoped.

I got out of the car and walked around the small town. I wandered into a little deli that had homemade breakfast sandwiches, snacks, and lots of cheeses and various homemade spreads. I bought some lunch and went back to my car, eating while googling all sorts of things that made my mind race.

I even contacted a lawyer with some of the advice I found online from people in a similar situation. I wasn't sure what was going to happen, but I needed a distraction.

My phone rang. It was Shaun.

"Cyn?" He sounded normal.

"What's happening?" I interrupted.

"I'm waiting to have a virtual court meeting. I told them what we're doing, and depending on the verdict, they might release me today."

I breathed a sigh of relief. I still had so many unanswered questions running through my head, but having some answers felt like a weight lifted off my shoulders. We hung up and I put my seat back, slipping into an uncomfortable but much needed sleep.

I woke up a couple of hours later to my phone ringing again. "I'm ready," he said. "Pull up to the front." I felt almost excited after starting the car. I was growing to like Shaun's presence; he had a lot of great ideas I would have never thought of myself.

He got into my car, and we both burst into bittersweet tears. "That fucking sucked," he said, pulling me into a tight hug. "That fucking sucked."

They banned Shaun from the national parks we'd already visited on our trip. We couldn't go back to Yellowstone, so we decided to head straight to Montana to hit Glacier National Park.

We had a long talk on the way, promising to be more careful and to change some of our habits. They'd confiscated the rocks Shaun collected from each national park, since taking the stones was a felony. They dropped the felony and fined him fifteen hundred dollars, which I paid for in thanks for his night in jail without me, wherein he'd added a misdemeanor for possession of drugs and paraphernalia to his record.

After testing the pills, it turned out our microdose mushrooms were also full of ecstasy and other drugs, apparently left over from the spice grinder the dealer had used to make them. Because of his good behavior and the reason we were out here, they lessened his punishment and got him out in a day, when they could have kept him longer for a more serious offense. Feeling both grateful and stupid, we headed northwest and hoped for brighter days ahead.

AUGUST 28, 2018

Glacier National Park, Montana

After another broken night of sleep, we got up early to reorganize my car that had been destroyed by the police search. We found some weed they'd left behind and got high to celebrate our luck.

On our way to Glacier National Park, we stopped at the Blackfoot Native American reservation to pay homage to my ancestors; my mom's family has Blackfoot blood. I stopped to get gas, and Shaun went inside to grab some snacks.

"Hey," I heard someone call out but didn't think anything of it. Then he whistled. "Hey!" the male voice said again, clearly trying to get my attention.

I turned around and stared at the guy. He rolled his window down and asked me how I was doing.

"I'm not interested." I turned back to the pump.

"I live jus' down the street," he said. "Common! Git in."

I ignored him.

"Dumb bitch," he snarled, peeling out of the parking lot.

I got in the car, a little shaken that this was the second time I was harassed while alone, and with less than a month in. It was disheartening and had me feeling grateful Shaun was still with me and not back in jail.

For the last ten years, I'd gone to most places with Wayne. Nobody bothered me with him around; they'd be stupid to try. I wasn't used to this life of getting harassed, and it was frustrating when all I wanted was to be left alone.

We left the reservation and continued to our campsite in the Two Medicine area of the park. We set up camp and had some daylight left, so we got a quick hike in to a serene waterfall with a surprise visit by a fox on the drive back.

The next morning, our campground neighbor asked if we'd heard the bear by our tent around 2 a.m. We exchanged glances and shook our heads.

"Yep, was rustling around right back there," he pointed to the left of our tent. "I made a real loud sound, and he ran away."

"Good thing we're heading to the next spot," I said as we packed up, although thinking something with an ability to kill me was just lurking around while I slept kind of excited me.

On our way to the new site, we pulled over on the side of the road. We'd seen a crowd. I'd learned there were usually animals near any gathering of people in the middle of nowhere.

Excited, I hopped out of the car.

"Come over," an older man waved at me. He was peering through a large telescope pointed at the looming mountain above.

"Grizzlies," he said.

I lowered my face to the lens. A mom and babies.

"Nine of 'em," he huffed. "We spotted nine so far."

I made my way down the line of binoculars, each one pointed to a different bear.

"Them males up there will eat the young if the mamas ain't paying attention."

I thought about how most young in the animal kingdom are

cast out into the world to live a solitary life. I thought I'd be better suited for that. It felt good to be disconnected from my past and not really know what was going on at home.

Cell service was hard to come by while living in national parks. I'd become completely ignorant to the rest of the world and utterly absorbed in my loss.

Shortly after Wayne died, I'd hid most of my friends online, especially those with happy lives. I resented the women who posted complaints about their husbands' business trips or weekend out with the guys. I didn't want to see engagements, wedding photos, or babies being born. I couldn't process how other people's lives went on, while mine had stopped.

This hopelessness consumed me as I watched the bears graze on berry bushes from afar. The lens got blurry when the tears I was desperately trying to contain dripped from my eyes.

I looked up, thanked the man, and got back in the car. We were on our way to hike a few trails before visiting the Logan Pass Visitor Center on Going to the Sun Road.

SHAUN

I'd been hiking almost all day every day for the last month, and it became my only solace. On the trail engulfed in nature, I was insignificant and small. Somehow, my problems didn't feel so enormous while standing alone in a valley surrounded by mountain peaks, waterfalls, wildlife, and babbling streams.

I accomplished more than I ever thought I could, hiking high elevations in short distances and forcing myself to keep going even when it hurt. I was losing weight, gaining muscle, and pushing my boundaries more every day.

We hiked four waterfall trails in Glacier National Park and chased the sunset over Saint Mary Lake. We were going horseback riding the next day, but Shaun and I had an argument, and he wouldn't talk to me.

I left camp and went for a short walk before it got dark, hoping to catch another moose during the dusk light.

I sat on a boulder alone, looking across the sparkling blue water, and began to cry. I wanted nothing more than to be here with Wayne. I missed his goofy smile and the way he'd educate me on lichens and fungi and all the different biology facts he could fit in during a walk in the woods. I missed the way we talked about—and to—the animals, giving them voices and creating stories about their lives. I missed his fun-loving nature, his gentle way with me even when I was being unreasonable and uptight. I missed the way he loved me despite my flaws. *I wish more than anything I was dealing with his flaws right now.*

Living in a compact SUV and a tent with another person isn't easy, especially when it's someone you haven't been close to for long. You learn a lot about each other in a short amount of time.

There was no escaping for me, except for the solo hikes I insisted on or private public bathroom time.

Shaun was fun, adventurous, encouraging, spontaneous… and slightly controlling, but that created a perfect match for someone who had no opinion and no direction. I adapted to his way of doing things, letting him take the lead on a lot of our decisions. I didn't care if I was dead or alive, so following his plans didn't bother me. His ideas were always better anyway. I'd tried to rearrange the car a few times, but he always redid every attempt I made. There were a lot of things I did that didn't seem to be good enough, but *I* wasn't good enough, so it felt normal.

He was supposed to fly back home after about three months. We figured we might be near Los Angeles by then, and I'd continue alone. He'd get another job, and I would finally get what I was yearning for: alone time.

I learned a lot from him, watching curiously as he expertly assembled and rigged things up that would make our lives easier. I was continuously impressed with the ideas he came up with, like building a frame with tent poles and covering it in a fleece blanket to trap heat over the mattress on freezing cold nights, or creating a hammock from a blanket to hold our phones so we could watch a movie on rainy days, or using a steel flint to make fire from a spark. He also always knew the way on the trail even if I was turned around, and he saved me from a few hairy areas.

On the extra hard days, he would set up a tissue dispenser for me to access the toilet paper when the crying was nonstop and leave me in the tent to grieve alone while he did his own thing. Sometimes he'd come back with KFC or Subway, and we'd spend the rest of the night watching old reruns he'd downloaded on his laptop as we binged on food we hadn't eaten in months.

Shaun was an expert at planning, finding the best hikes in the area and putting together an itinerary with a glance at the map. Our days were booked solid from dawn till dusk, as we took advantage of every last drop of sunlight to see as much as we could before starting all over again the next day.

In a way, we made a great team. I didn't have the energy to plan even a day ahead, and he liked things his way. I went along, floating around high all day and feeling like both the luckiest person alive to be able to experience nature this personally while also feeling like I'd suffered the worst thing a human could endure. It was confusing and always changing.

Still, the main point of my trip never left my mind. I wanted to be alone. I wanted to rely on myself. I yearned for silent, judgment-free days where all I had to worry about was how I'd get water and where I'd pee. I didn't want to be responsible for someone else's emotions. I couldn't be.

"He has no money," Shaun's mom had said to me through the open passenger's side window in broken English in the parking lot of their apartment complex as I was picking him up for our departure. Only a few days prior, he'd told me he had ten thousand dollars. Suddenly, he'd told me he had to loan his parents most of it for an unspoken reason. "When will you come back?"

I glanced at Shaun then back at her. "I'm not sure. We'll figure it out as we go," I said before saying our goodbyes and driving away. I didn't ask him any more questions.

I was now funding life for the both of us, but it wasn't costing much more than if I were alone, I justified. It was just extra food and maybe a few other things here and there he would need along the way. The added expense was more than worth it, and I felt like I was paying him back for all the help he'd given me in the beginning when I could barely function.

My tears brought me back to the morning before. We hit the visitor center, and I browsed the vertical turntables with all different types of magnets for sale. This was something Wayne and I had started collecting on all our travels, and I was continuing in his honor. I bought a magnet at every national park and planned to arrange them on a chalkboard if I ever had my own place again.

Shaun had shown me a Glacier National Park pin. "This would be cool for me to collect."

"Yeah. Nice, small, and not illegal," I joked.

"No, for real," he said. "These could replace the rocks I was collecting."

"Go for it." I ran my fingers over a carved, wooden mountain scene.

"Will you get it for me?" he asked.

I turned away from the colorful magnets and looked at him, confused. *He was serious?*

"What? No, I'm already getting magnets for myself at each park. You can get them."

"But I don't have any money," he insisted.

"Well, I'm sorry, but I'm already spending a lot, and this just isn't a necessity," I replied, taken aback but also feeling bad for his situation.

"And *that* is…?" he gestured to the magnet in my hand. "You get magnets, but what do I get?"

My eyes darted around nervously at the families around us, wondering if I was the only one hearing our interaction. I felt like he was a child, and I was a mother saying no at the toy store. He seemed like he was about to throw a tantrum, but I also felt incredibly guilty. *What's one more thing?* I reasoned. *I should just get it.*

Before I could, he turned around and left. I left the pin and paid for my magnet, replaying the scene in my head, wondering if he was just having a bad day or if we were just spending way too much time together.

"Are you okay?" I asked once I got into the car. I was met with no eye contact and silence.

After realizing I wasn't going to get an answer, I stopped staring at the back of his head and drove back to our campsite. He wouldn't talk to me even after we got back, when we normally would have been deciding what type of soup or noodles we were going to heat up that night for dinner.

We went about the rest of the evening, sitting five feet away from each other in silence. I wanted to laugh several times; the situation seemed so comical, so petty, so unnecessary. This was the last thing I wanted to spend my energy, and my trip, on. My inner laughter turned to anger and longing the more I stewed on it, because I knew I wouldn't have to deal with this if I were alone, or if I were with Wayne.

I jumped off the boulder with the moonlight guiding my path as I walked back to camp quicker than usual. I climbed into the tent immediately, too exhausted to do anything else. To my surprise, Shaun wasn't inside. I laid down and tried reading one of my widow books I'd brought. I still had trouble concentrating and couldn't focus enough to absorb any of the words on the page.

Frustrated and tired, I sighed and closed the book. I tried to get comfy on the ground, but my thin sleeping pad wasn't cutting it tonight. I had no idea what time it was. My phone had died hours earlier, but it didn't matter. Time melted together, and I had zero responsibility. It didn't matter what time I fell asleep or what time I woke up. It was all the same.

I heard my car door slam shut and the zipper behind me open. Shaun got into his sleeping bag and went to sleep without saying a word.

SEPTEMBER 1, 2018

Glacier National Park, Montana

I opened the glovebox and grabbed the blue plastic joint container I'd started using to carry Wayne's ashes. It was the perfect temporary urn. Small, stable. I could bring him with me and release a tiny capful on mountain summits, in waterfalls and oceans, mixed through sand dunes and throughout rainforests. I was sprinkling Wayne everywhere I went, and it never got any easier.

I slipped him into my pocket and got out of the car. We were going horseback riding today, and Shaun was talking to me again, acting like nothing had ever happened yesterday. As long as we weren't fighting, I didn't care. I definitely wasn't going to disturb the peace by bringing it up.

We climbed onto our horses, Gilligan and Beaufort, and rode through dried-up lakes and forested meadows with mountainous backdrops. We learned about the area's terrain from our guide, Ashley, who kept giggling at Shaun's remarks and laughed harder at his jokes than anyone I'd ever heard.

After our ride, we went on our first guided hike to Grinnell Lake, and I released Wayne's ashes into the clear water with the backdrop of waterfalls cascading down the cliffs above.

Our guide recognized red, juicy thimbleberries growing on the bushes on the side of the trail, and we picked and ate them confidently, our eyes wide at the sweetness and tartness of the wild berries.

We didn't drive back to camp until late. On the way, a fox ran adjacent to our car, using the headlights as his guide. He stopped and pounced, producing a mouse he promptly ate in the middle of the road while we watched. I felt like we'd contributed to the circle of life—even if just a little.

SEPTEMBER 3, 2018

It was our last day in Montana, and we rounded out our grizzly bear sightings to nineteen after seeing a mom and two cubs on a nearby mountainside. We got a piece of peanut butter and huckleberry pie at a little roadside stand with pink, painted wood panels and watched wild horses run by as we savored the sweet and silky treat.

It was time to head to Washington if we still wanted to take advantage of the mountain hikes without the threat of snow at higher elevations.

I bought a book before the trip with a list of free campsites in every state. We were going to try our luck by stopping at public land a little outside of Spokane, a bigger city in eastern Washington, for the night. Park campsites were getting expensive, and I needed to start saving money where I could.

After driving for what felt like days, we turned left onto a dusty, sandy side road. It was pitch black, and our headlights scared off a few porcupines we came across on the way. Prickly bushes grew everywhere with no civilization in sight. Our eyes were drooping and drowsy as we drove further into the brush.

We finally arrived at a gate we thought should lead us to the BLM land, but it was locked.

Exhausted and annoyed, we could either pitch our tent by the closed gate and hope nobody came by or find another campground. Neither of us had cell service, and our only guide was the free book that led us astray in the first place. It was 1 a.m., we had a long day ahead, and we were both exhausted and bickering.

"Let's just set up the tent here," I suggested. "I don't think we can make it to another campground right now. I have no idea where the next one is, and I'm seriously so exhausted."

"Are you for real?" Shaun asked, staring back at me. "Here?"

That's all the direction I needed. I got into the driver's seat and unwillingly drove back to the highway, resenting my inability to make decisions. An hour and a half later, we checked into a hotel near the Coulee Dam and got high in the parking lot before slipping into a much-needed deep sleep, cradled by the comforts of a room, a private bathroom with shower, and a real bed for the first time in over a month.

SEPTEMBER 6, 2018

North Cascades National Park, Washington

The last few days were full of adventure as we continued west. Driving through the North Cascades was like a dream. The jagged peaks broke into the sky above and loomed over the twisting and guardrail-less mountain roads. There seemed to be waterfalls everywhere I turned, cascading down the sides of the hard rock that lined Highway 20.

I'd been to most states by then, having road-tripped and camped with my family as a child and into my adult years with Wayne. But this was my first time in Washington, and I'd clearly underestimated the beauty and wild energy the Evergreen State exuded.

We spent our days hiking and stopping at overlooks that displayed lakes with water so blue, I couldn't believe it was natural. We had simple meals dwarfed by giant, ancient trees and combed the visitor center, taking time to explore every easily accessible inch of one of the least-visited parks in the country. Most of North Cascades National Park is so wild that you can only visit by hiking the trails that run through it.

Pulling over at one of the more scenic picnic areas, I got out of the car and lugged out the portable stove and fuel canister. We had one cast iron skillet where we did all the cooking, whether it be ramen noodles or a fireside breakfast.

Dehydrated meals got old fast, and eating a hot meal that didn't start as little flakes felt like a luxury. I made a few trips to and from the car, carrying all the supplies we'd need for lunch. I went to grab the paper towels, but noticed the roll was torn. Not thinking much of it, I grabbed a few sheets and brought them to the splintery, damp picnic bench.

I warmed up the leftover rotisserie chicken we'd had for dinner on a recent night and wrapped it in flour tortillas. We ate quickly, and Shaun started planning our route for the next few days while I pretended to listen. We were heading to Seattle soon, the first big city on the itinerary. At first, I protested; I wanted nothing to do with city life or the people living in it. I didn't want to deal with traffic, crowds, or remember that life kept moving even though the most important person on the planet was dead. This wasn't the goal of my trip. Plus, cities are expensive.

After arguing about it for a while, Shaun convinced me we'd be missing an opportunity if we left cities out of the trip. He wanted to try all the different food in each region. I quickly gave up and decided to just enjoy the adventure, no matter where it took me.

I packed up, and we headed out in silence. I heard some rustling noises in the back but figured it was a rogue grocery bag shifting with the moving car. We were changing campsites today, continuing southwest, and I was tired from the on-the-go lifestyle and driving. I was looking forward to a chill evening of watching reruns on Shaun's laptop until we passed out—but first, we had to set up camp.

We circled the empty North Cascades campground a few times, eager to find the best, most secluded spot. This was one of my favorite parts of getting to a new place. The process brought back so many memories of driving through campsites with my parents, just to look at everyone's setup.

I decided on a small spot away from everything else but close enough to the wooden outhouse for an easy walk during the night if needed. The forests in Washington are unlike anything I'd ever experienced. The trees are hundreds and hundreds of years old, looming so tall over my head that I felt dizzy when I looked up. The trunks are thicker than ten normal trees from the Midwest put together, draped with soft, wet moss that blankets everything in a layer of green velvet.

Downed trees lay everywhere, acting as nurse logs to new life and feeding the fragrant soil below. There were hollow trees, charred trees, twisted trees, trees with intricate root systems exposed, large stumps, and bare trees with bald eagle nests.

The mist and fog Washington is famous for cast an ominous and eerie glow over the forests, creating droplets of water crystals on the large, full ferns that covered the forest floor. Little creeks broke up the mountainous ground, guiding cold, clear water down to lakes, streams, and oceans. Wooden bridges built by hikers or park rangers with the wood from the forest dotted the landscape, providing access over rushing waterfalls and fast rivers.

Everything is different here, I thought. *It smells different. It sounds different. It feels different.* Even the ground felt different, like a sponge waiting to suck me up with every step. Hiking here was like walking on clouds surrounded by a mysterious organic grove, where something magical awaited with every bend of the trail.

I started unloading our gear. A two-person tent we used when we were staying just a couple of nights, or if we didn't have room for the eight-person tent. A tarp to line the bottom of the tent with. Two sleeping pads, two sleeping bags and two pillows. A rainfly, the rusty hatchet, some tent stakes, and a couple of fleece throw blankets. The process was simple but quick, my favorite way of doing things.

I cleared a spot for the tent and pitched it quickly, a self-proclaimed expert at setting up camp by now. I could get the tent standing in thirty seconds and the inside set up in a few minutes. I didn't like spending too much time setting things up for our camping. They were just going to be torn down, forgotten the next day and in the past. I grabbed a couple of lanterns and threw them into the tent with some other essentials.

We'd be in the North Cascades for two more nights before heading to Seattle and Sea-Tac International Airport in Tacoma to catch our flight to Anchorage. I'd already been to Glacier Bay National Park and explored the coastal towns with my dad earlier that spring and was craving to be back in Alaska's wild embrace.

Washington feels like a mini-Alaska, I decided. *Not so grand, but easier to access and cheaper to visit.* There was something different about this state. I was pulled in, like I had roots there, even though I'd never been. I felt like I belonged.

It was getting dark and we'd had a late lunch, so we decided to hang out in the car for the night before sleeping in the tent.

My car had become my home. I felt most at peace there, knowing everything I needed to survive was tucked carefully just an arm's length away. I didn't need much. I craved a minimalist life. Everything else in my life felt so noisy and hard around me that I couldn't add the additional confusion of material possessions to the chaos. I had two duffel bags stuffed with leggings, hiking socks, thermals, a hat, gloves, tank tops, hoodies, jackets, a couple of weeks' worth of underwear, one pair of jeans, and one or two non-hiking tops I washed at laundromats with the stash of quarters I saved up every so often.

I'd brought a pair of waterproof hiking shoes, a pair of trail runners, and some flip-flops. Baby wipes were a necessity, since showers were hard to come by. Deodorant was a must, and I brushed my teeth with toothpaste and water from a gallon jug. My endless supply of dry shampoo brought a false sense of cleanliness when I went too long without washing my ashy, thin hair that had fallen out in clumps a few months after Wayne died. I brought some mascara and eyeliner but couldn't imagine ever needing it. I no longer owned a razor.

I loved the freedom of not caring what I looked or smelled like. After all, it truly didn't matter. Keeping up my appearance after Wayne died was something I just didn't prioritize; I was too busy breathing. Food, water, survival. That's all I *really* had to care about.

Everything else in the car consisted of food, water, camping and sleeping gear, first aid, and random tools—enough supplies to ensure long-term survival if something were to happen on the road. It had only been a month, but I felt like I'd been living in my car for years. Shaun had tied up photos of the cats on the visors, and Wayne's powdered bones were in the glovebox. The most important things in my life were with me, but they were just representations of the warm bodies I used to spend my nights with. Still, I felt slight comfort knowing I'd once had a family of my own, and I had the evidence to prove it. Not that I needed to convince anyone but myself.

I settled into the passenger's seat as Shaun set up his laptop on the dashboard. We were rewatching *Breaking Bad*, my all-time favorite series. I could only watch reruns of things I'd already digested; anything else took too much brain power to absorb or care about.

I'd started to doze off after the second episode when I felt something warm move across my bare foot, followed by something hairy, thin, and cold. My eyes widened and I swung open the car door, moving both at warp speed and in slow motion. I was silent, but I knew I should have been screaming.

"A MOUSE!" I hissed at Shaun in a half whisper, half yell.

"What? Stop…get in."

"The torn paper towels…the rustling. It all makes sense now!"

I stood outside, frozen, not sure what to do. Shaun sat and stared at me. A rodent had just scurried across my foot and was living in my car with us. I felt so unclean and…violated!

"Get out!" I yelled, throwing open the back door and taking our belongings out of the car.

I went to open the plastic cooler and noticed new claw marks I hadn't seen before. The lid creaked loudly as I slowly opened it just enough to peek inside. Bracing myself, I squinted my eyes at mouse droppings all over the bottom of the cooler. The crackers were ripped open. I had been feeding and hosting him for days, it seemed.

I grabbed the cooler and threw it and all the contents away at the dumpster by the outhouse. "We have to sanitize everything. We need mouse traps, and we have to keep all our belongings outside of the car."

We'd relied on the car to keep our things safe from the elements and animals, and now everything would be subjected to the outside world.

Exhausted and annoyed, we hauled our duffel bags and soft materials into the tiny tent, taking up way more room than we had to sleep. All the rest would need to be locked inside the bear box at our campsite.

After we finished emptying the car, we opened all the doors and turned on all the lights. Shaun grabbed a trekking pole and started poking around under the seats. A little gray mouse ran to the other side.

We grabbed a flashlight and peered under the back seat. The light illuminated a large pile of shredded paper towels under the middle of the seat. A nest. A second gray mouse.

A mouse nest in my car. My house.

If they weren't taking up residence in my already crowded living space, I would be taking pictures and naming them. They were so cute—little gray bodies with huge ears, little pink noses, and curious faces that looked at me with fear in their beady eyes.

Tears of frustration welled up in my own eyes, knowing mice in King County, Washington, could carry a deadly disease called hantavirus that can take weeks to show symptoms.

We closed up the car, mice in tow, and drove to the nearest general store miles away. I put my legs and feet up on the dashboard, shuddering at the thought of the mouse tail between my toes. We left the store with rodent traps, peanut butter, rubber gloves and bleach, and headed back to the campsite, prepared to take action.

We removed the nest from under the back seat, placed cotton balls soaked with peppermint oil around the car, and cleaned every surface before setting two traps.

We only had two nights to get rid of our new roommates before I would be leaving my car at the airport for seven days. By the time we got back from Alaska, the car would be destroyed if they remained inside.

I lay awake for half the night, squished into the nylon walls of the tent by half the car's contents, with condensation rubbing against my face. The urge to look at the mouse traps was unreal, but navigating through this mess was preventing me from moving a muscle.

I fell asleep thinking about a little mouse family just trying to stay warm and dry, but squeezing to death instead.

SEPTEMBER 7, 2018

I stared down at the triumphant trap. The dead mouse's eyes bulged out of its skull, four times bigger than they were the night before when we made eye contact from under the seat. Its mouth was slightly ajar, displaying its long, yellow buckteeth.

This wasn't the first animal we'd killed on the road. Shaun hit a golden eagle on the highway, causing it to tumble and somersault at superspeed behind us, feathers flying everywhere as I'd watched in horror in the rearview mirror.

"Where's the other one?" I wondered, guilt rising in my throat at thinking about the mouse's spouse grieving over the dead carcass, the way I had done nine months earlier.

"This probably scared it away," Shaun said, picking up the body by the trap. He tossed it into the garbage, and we left the second trap intact just in case. We both hopped in the car, which was still empty from our purge the previous night. We decided to take a chance by leaving our gear in our tent and bear box during our hike, hoping nobody came by interested in what we had.

We were conquering Cascade Pass, a seven-mile hike with eighteen hundred feet of elevation gain. Although this wasn't the steepest trail we'd hiked, it boasted thirty-seven switchbacks and most of its gain within the first three miles.

I wasn't a professional hiker by any means, even though I'd moved my body more in the last month than I ever had. We covered an average of ten miles per day, sometimes less and sometimes more. New calluses formed on my once-soft heels, allowing me to cover longer distances when coupled with my recently developed muscles.

After we drove for what seemed like endless miles on a gravel road littered with monstrous potholes and massive old-growth trees, the mountains started towering more than four thousand feet over our heads. We arrived at the parking lot, which was only partially full on a weekday in September.

I grabbed my pack from the car and looked up. We were in a circular lot, surrounded by evergreens and engulfed by Johannesburg Mountain, worth the view even if we didn't hike up. It was a warm, clear day, perfect for viewing the sweeping, vast mountain vistas.

As we made our way through the forested ascent, the mountains cradling the trees provided shade and shelter from the midday sun. I was no stranger to switchbacks since working my way northwest where the peaks had gotten taller and more demanding. But I'd never done anything like this. The hike seemed incredibly monotonous, with half of my brain focused on misery and aching legs and the other half reminding me this was the easiest thing I'd ever done. *Dead, dead, dead, dead,* I chanted in my head with each step. Wayne was dead, and I was exploring these beautiful mountains, feeling sorry for myself.

I hate myself, I thought, using the disgust as fuel to keep going. *I'm disgusting, mean, selfish. I wouldn't cuddle with Wayne, and I left for work, and he died. I didn't even cuddle him when I got home. I couldn't even do that! Now he can never experience anything like this. I'm only here because he's gone.*

Every sarcastic remark or snarky moment Wayne and I had shared replayed through my mind, amplified by the reasoning behind them. Such stupid arguments. Ridiculous fights about money and work and things so insignificant in hindsight but feeling so intense in the moment.

I hated him. I hated him for dying on me and leaving me here alone. I hated him for not giving me one last chance to tell him how much he meant to me, even though I knew he already knew. I hated him for not taking his sickness more seriously, and I hated myself for it too.

I hated him for loving me so much—making me feel a way I knew I'd never experience again. I hated him for making me long for it. Most of all, I hated myself for hating him and then went right back to loving him.

My head was pounding and sweat dripped off my back, pressing back into my skin when my pack rubbed my shirt with every step. Aware I wasn't hydrating enough, I stopped to take a break.

I sucked the cold water through the rubber straw in my bag, which was attached to my strap with a little clip. Each switchback stretched longer and longer, with no end in sight.

I thought back to the Badlands in South Dakota. It was hot, I had been fat, and I just didn't want to do it. I remembered glancing up at the glaring sun and massive incline with no shade. *I don't have to force myself to do anything I don't want to do,* I'd told myself to justify it.

I'd turned around at the trailhead that day in the Badlands. I stayed in the tent and cried, full of self-loathing and hatred for my life, wondering if I should just end it all there. But it was the last time I gave up. From that moment on, I hiked short and long trails, easy and strenuous, boiling hot and freezing cold and everything in between.

Despite how much I wanted to quit, I didn't. I finished every hike I started, no matter how miserable some of them were. With my thighs screaming, my head pounding, my feet aching, and my chest exploding, all I needed to do was think of Wayne.

Trekking on, I hoped we just had a few more switchbacks to get through before making it above the tree line. We hadn't met very many people on the trail, and I couldn't wait to sit at the summit alone.

"Suck in your gut," Shaun said from behind me. "You should work on your posture. When you're walking, tighten your core."

I did.

The green pines faded away, and the landscape transformed into an enormous rock field, introducing breathtaking vistas complete with open slopes and hanging glaciers. Marmots and pikas chirped at us as we navigated our already tired legs through crevices and boulders.

The trail made a few final bends and opened to the pass, displaying a lush valley below dotted with impressive peaks, glaciers, and lakes.

The ridge from Johannesburg Mountain connects to Mixup Peak and Magic Mountain, with Cache Glacier in between. The horizon displayed glacier-dotted lower slopes and the snowy summit ridge of El Dorado Peak. Just beyond and above the pass, it's common to spot deer, mountain goat, and bear in the wildflower and blueberry fields.

I sat on the almost manmade-looking rock facing the picturesque scene and took a long, deep breath. Goosebumps covered my skin while I took it all in. I felt amazing in the moment, absorbing the adrenaline rush and endorphin boost racing through my body.

This is the only thing that makes me feel alive. Being present, here and now. The mountains heal me. Nothing else on this Earth matters. My problems aren't real; my thoughts don't matter. So many things are outside of my control.

I can walk. I can take one step and then another step. I can repeat that until I reach a goal, and then I will feel accomplished. That's what I can handle.

SEPTEMBER 11, 2018

Alaska

The plane landed roughly on the runway, shaking me awake from a broken, unproductive sleep. Seattle is a completely different world than I'd been living in the last six weeks, and I was exhausted after trying to blend in with "normal" people.

It felt funny playing tourist, like I was living some type of double life or lie. I was supposed to be living the minimalistic life in nature—not indulging in biscuit sandwiches and Russian pastries from Pike Place Market and showering more than once a week.

I booked a cheap Airbnb outside the city with a washer and dryer so we could take advantage of our mini "vacation" and get some necessities done before leaving for Alaska, but the washer was broken so we had to use a laundromat anyway. We ate our weight in cookies, ice cream, pasta, and breakfast sandwiches and napped in a real bed with a TV. It was a welcome break from SUV living.

Landing in Alaska, I opened the sliding, white window shade of our airplane and peeked outside. Mountains engulfed the airport, a 360-degree view of unparalleled beauty. *Even the ugly parts of Alaska are beautiful*, I thought.

We arrived at our rental home after picking up the rental car, and to my surprise, our address was "Weimer Road." I smiled at the coincidence, wondering why I hadn't noticed the destination address before we arrived.

I'd never planned to take Wayne's last name, even if he didn't die. I loved my full name, and it suited me well. He never had an issue with it and encouraged me to remain independent.

Thanks, Wayne, I said to myself, taking the address as a sign that he was still with me.

I opened the door to the tiny but neat apartment, another "luxury stay" I hadn't planned for, but it wasn't much more expensive than a campsite anyway. Somehow, we had a packed itinerary for the week, and I was grateful for the spotty cell service we'd snuck into our trip while planning from the visitor center back in Yellowstone.

We were headed to Denali National Park first, which would include a four-hour drive from Anchorage, an eight-hour bus tour through the park, and a four-hour drive home all in the same day.

I collapsed with exhaustion, knowing tomorrow was going to be an early and long day but grateful for the temporary distraction from my thoughts.

SEPTEMBER 12, 2018

Denali National Park, Alaska

There's one road from Anchorage to Denali National Park, Route 3, which is also the main route to Fairbanks. The road was desolate and empty, rewarding us with expansive views from sunrise to sunset.

The autumn colors came alive at the same time as the sun, bursting into view as dawn turned into morning and quickly transformed into afternoon. Denali holds six million acres of wild land, starting at a relatively low elevation through forest and high alpine tundra and snowy mountains. As North America's tallest peak at over twenty thousand feet and the third most prominent and isolated peak on Earth after Mount Everest and Aconcagua, it towers over anything I'd seen up close.

Glaciers etch out 16 percent of the park, moving away from the mountain and melting into creeks and rivers that eventually spill out into the ocean. The only way to drive through the entire length of Denali National Park's only road is through a bus tour the park provides, with the chance to spot grizzly and black bears, wolves, caribou, moose, coyotes, lynx, sheep, bald eagles, Arctic ground squirrels, red squirrels, foxes, and marmots.

We arrived at the park entrance early and checked in at the visitor center to browse the gift shop before boarding the bus for the next eight hours. We'd packed some lunch and snacks for the ride, and I was looking forward to getting comfortable while losing myself in a foreign land wilder than I could imagine.

After boarding the bus, I gazed out of the oversized windows and listened as the guide rattled off facts about the land. He shared how, for thousands of years, Alaskan natives had lived on this land, using resources for food, shelter, clothing, transportation, and trade. The name *Denali* can mean "the tall one" or "mountain-big."

We made a couple of stops along the road, including a longer one so we could opt to take a short hike around one of the overlooks. I climbed off the bus with Wayne's ashes in my pocket, eager to spread him in such an untouched, wild place. Only about 30 percent of Denali's visitors get to see the mountain, since it's often covered by clouds, especially in the summer. I was part of the vast majority who didn't get to see the peak but felt its looming presence anyway.

It was windy and pleasant as I stepped onto the vast but intimate trail. I was surrounded by red, orange, and yellow bushes and plants, painted over rolling hills and open vistas. Crystal clear creeks snaked off every which way, creating natural white noise that was better than any radio station or podcast series I was used to back home.

I took a deep breath and tried to fill my body with the beauty. I opened the cap to the blue joint container and stuck my fingers into Wayne's powdery bones. Rubbing my thumb and index finger together, I crushed up the bigger chunks to a finer texture and imagined the dust I was touching was his hand instead of ground calcium.

I tipped over the smooth container slowly, only allowing a few pieces to fall to the ground at first. A gust of wind picked up my hair and swirled it around my face, taking me by surprise and causing me to rock back and forth while I tried to stabilize my feet on the rocky ground.

The rest of the ashes came out quickly, but instead of blowing into the wind and out of my life like they usually did, the dusty cloud suddenly changed direction and hit me in the face, covering my blue fleece jacket and black leggings. Instinctively, I started to wipe them away and immediately felt guilty, deciding to leave the smears of death on my clothes and cheeks. I walked back to the bus feeling closer to Wayne than I had in months.

Hours passed and I was glued to the windows, unblinking as the fairytale-like scenery blurred by. We saw the Alaska state bird, a willow ptarmigan. Five moose ran by at different times during the drive, and caribou, sheep, and porcupines rounded out our animal sightings for the day.

The sun was starting to set when we began the four-hour drive back to Anchorage, casting the jagged mountains in pinks, reds, and corals. I'd never seen a more spectacular sunset, something I didn't think would peak until we hit the ocean on the West Coast.

Two hours into the drive, we both became too exhausted to continue and pulled over at a small gas station in the middle of nowhere to get a few hours of sleep before driving the rest of the way. I reclined my seat as far as it would go and tried to find a comfortable spot for my head on the hard plastic door.

I felt naked in this bright blue rental car, a Ford Fiesta with a large "no smoking" sticker across the dashboard. It didn't contain my entire life in one, easy-to-reach space or hide me from the rest of the world with tinted windows. I had no pillow and blanket, no Icicle or Goose hanging from the mirror, no change of clothes. No familiar smells and no rodent roommates. I drifted off thinking how funny it was to long for a home that wasn't really a home, that living in a car means homelessness to most people, and how that really wasn't funny at all.

SEPTEMBER 13, 2018

Kenai Fjords National Park, Alaska

After eating a quick breakfast, we were on our way south to Seward to explore Kenai Fjords National Park—winding our way through the Turnagain Arm, a dramatic shoreline at the base of the Chugach Mountains—when two black and white swans flew parallel to the car.

"Swans!" I shouted, adding the animal to my journal. I got excited every time we saw something new on the road. I planned on tallying up all the different species at the end, whenever that was.

After a few bends in the highway, two large brown shapes came into view, and I screamed out, "Moose!" laughing, as I was now not so surprised to see them.

We were on our way to a boat ride through the Kenai Peninsula, an icefield with outflowing glaciers, coastal fjords, sea caves, and islands. Known for jagged cliffs, tumbling glaciers, pristine waters, and abundant wildlife, the fjords are glacial valleys that have been submerged below sea level by rising sea levels and sinking land.

This was my first chance at seeing orca whales, which had been my all-time favorite animal ever since I was a little girl who fell in love with *Free Willy* and the artwork of Lisa Frank. I always dreamed of seeing them in the wild after coming face to face with them at Sea World in Ohio in the nineties before they closed, when it was still widely acceptable to take your family there to support the exploitation of wild animals.

I had countless orca stuffed animals, including one that was bigger than me that my dad got with tickets from a jackpot he'd won at a local arcade. At age six, I favored a heavy rubber orca I played with in the bath and took in swimming pools and lakes, eventually losing it in Lake Erie during a summer camping trip with my family.

I'd swam around and cried, opening my eyes under the dirty water, using my feet to detect anything other than sand. No luck. I doggy-paddled up to anyone around and told them if they found a rubber whale, it was mine and I really needed him back. I looked over the horizon helplessly, the lake resembling an endless ocean while large, strong waves bounced me around. I was about to give up, picturing the black and white whale swimming one hundred miles away by now, when a man held his arms up triumphantly, yelling for me to come back. He had my whale in his hand, and I never took it out of the house again.

The boat zoomed by sea lions, mountain goats, jellyfish, porpoise, seals, and humpbacks, but no orca whales. We went from glacier to glacier, passing by Bear Glacier, the largest and longest in the park.

As our boat stood still and the silence of the sea took over, the enormous white and blue glacier rose above me like an ice castle ready to defend its borders. In what seemed like an act of war, it shed an enormous chunk, sending a piece of ice five times the size of the ship into the water below. Wide-eyed and open-mouthed, I gawked at the glacier, speechless from what I'd witnessed. A few short seconds later, a deafening, thunderous roar bounced off the sea stacks and caverns, cracking like a whip after a lightning strike in the dog days of a Midwestern summer.

A few small waves formed at the base of the glacier and bounced their way to our boat, the power of it all rocking us ever so slightly.

We were on our way back to the shore to disembark when the loudspeaker announced three orca whales on the starboard side of the boat.

I jumped out of my seat, my heart pounding with excitement. I was finally going to witness these majestic creatures in person. The butterflies in my stomach felt foreign as I fought my way up to the deck.

The area was crowded with everyone else doing the same thing I was trying to do, people much taller than me with expensive cameras and more confidence and assertiveness to push to the front.

I couldn't see much, but I got a few glimpses of their shiny black backs as they breached the surface for air before disappearing as quickly as they'd arrived.

SEPTEMBER 15, 2018

Lake Clark National Park, Alaska

I climbed onto the tiny floatplane, feeling energized by a lazy rest day the previous day.

We were on our way to Lake Clark National Park, four million acres of remote beauty established in 1980. There are no roads to the park, and it can only be accessed by boat or air. The area protects alpine tundra, glaciers, glacial lakes, salmon-bearing rivers, two volcanoes, and rainforests along the coastline of the Cook Inlet. Sockeye salmon play a major role in the ecosystem and the local economy, which means large populations of brown bear feed on the spawning salmon in the summer months.

We were in the air for about an hour, soaring over the Alaskan wilderness, which was exploding with color before being covered in snow for the next eight months. It was just me, the pilot, and Shaun. Lake Clark National Park only gets about twenty-three thousand visitors per year, so it made sense that we were alone. He talked about the area as we passed by moose and other wildlife, and rivers that snaked along the multicolored ground and dumped out into the ocean under mountains that felt so close but so unreachable.

The turquoise water of Crescent Lake came into view, with scenic glimpses of Redoubt Volcano and the snowcapped Chigmit Mountains surrounding us. The trees were green, yellow, gold, orange, and red, dotting the shoreline and mountainside above. The floatplane landed effortlessly in the crystal-clear lake, its motor disrupting the deafening silence. I felt like I was on a spaceship and had landed on another planet. Not a soul was around. I was the only person alive.

We pulled up to the shoreline, and I hopped out. My feet landed on smooth, colored pebbles, and I sunk into the earth as I looked up around me. The red plane seemed so out of place in the painting-like scenery, but somehow it fit. It was a cloudy day, which made the piercing, teal water and little plane stand out even more from the gray sky.

A pontoon boat was tied to an old wooden dock that looked like it hadn't been maintained in years. The pilot gave us yellow rain ponchos and gestured to the boat, warning us this was the safest way to travel the area because of the dense vegetation and number of bears roaming in search of the last few pounds of salmon before fall and winter set in.

He got back into his plane and told us he'd be back in a few hours to pick us up. Our boat guide would be there soon.

I walked onto the rickety pontoon, making my way to the end to look out across the sparkling lake and foggy mountains. I thought I saw something move on the other side of the lake. Squinting for a better look, I realized I definitely saw something move on the other side of the lake.

I called Shaun over, silently but frantically, now thankful for the old boat acting as our safety island. A huge brown bear emerged from the brush, coming our way but still far enough away that I was hypnotized and not at all scared. He walked parallel with the shore, checking every so often to see if there was anything of interest to explore in the water.

The boat started rocking, breaking me out of a several-minute gaze and tearing my head away from the bear across the lake.

"Howdy." A tall man with rubber boots up to his knees stepped onto the boat from the shore. "I'll be taking you out today. Have you ever done anything like this before?"

I shook my head as he untied the boat from the dock. We floated away from the shore, getting closer to the bear but somehow safer and more protected.

"Y'all came at an interesting time," he said. "By now, most of the salmon are dead, and the bears are scrounging for the last of their calories before winter. But they're still here, as you can see."

We glided past the huge bear on the shore and turned into an open area of the lake, revealing a much bigger body of water than I'd anticipated. We followed a couple of other bears hunting for salmon on a rocky vista and passed a pair getting territorial about their fishing spots. They got up on their hind legs and swiped at each other before getting back down on all fours to run down the shore. There was clearly a winner, and he wasn't about to give up his spot for a rookie. We slowed down in the middle of the lake as the alpha submerged himself in the calm water, falling backwards onto his back with his feet in the air. He didn't seem to care we were only about a hundred feet away, prying into his life like humans do.

He resurfaced a few seconds later, a bright pink salmon between his strong jaws and large teeth. He sat down on the lake bottom, and only his head popped out from the water. He tore into the healthy fish, its bones crunching beneath the extreme power of it all. He chewed and made eye contact with me as I sat in awe of our planet and my life. The cracking bones echoed from the mountains back down to the lake and wove in between the sound of tearing flesh, as the turquoise water surrounding the bear turned purple with the bright red blood of the salmon.

I grabbed Wayne's ashes from my pocket and discreetly emptied the contents into the lake without anyone noticing. The cloud floated and sparkled before dispersing into the gentle waves of our boat as we made our way to the other side of the shore.

We immediately spotted two more bears: a mama with her fuzzy, toddler-aged cub. The cub danced around boulders and downed trees, trying to pick fights with her and anything else it came into contact with.

When we docked, we walked up the stairs of an old log cabin with a stone chimney. Inside, there was a dining table, and a bookshelf full of books on Alaska and photos of bears and salmon.

The cabin was warm and dry inside and smelled of charred wood and pine. We sat at the table, and a woman came out from the kitchen with two plates of Caesar salad, a side of jasmine rice, and a meaty piece of glazed salmon.

"This is the same salmon the bears were munching on outside," she said, smiling at the look of disbelief and uncertainty on my face.

"I've never actually had salmon before," I said, remembering back to when Wayne would hold out his fork for me to try his seafood and wouldn't stop until I did, begrudgingly. It was always the same—fishy and salty like the sea, a taste I never grew to love despite my silent protests.

"This isn't just any old salmon. This is the freshest, most delicious Alaskan sockeye salmon you will ever have the chance to eat."

I nodded and took a bite, feeling extremely close to Wayne, nature, and my bear friends. Although ours had a sweet maple glaze on top of a seared skin, I understood why the bears liked it so much. It was juicy and savory and sweet and moist, melting in my mouth with every bite.

After a few drinks and ice cream for dessert, we got back into our pontoon to watch more bears before heading back to meet the pilot.

On our way, the mama bear and her fuzzy cub appeared again at the water's edge. He was trying to play with her, but she was on a mission. He disappeared from her sight and only came back when he realized she was getting too far away to see.

There was that feeling again. I felt like both the luckiest and unluckiest person alive—watching these bears, knowing I was one of the twenty-three thousand people per year who made it to this part of the Earth. But I was only here because of the worst thing that had ever happened to me.

We got back on the plane, and it was smooth sailing for about thirty minutes before I heard, "He isn't supposed to be on this flight path…." from the headphones cuffing my ears.

"What the hell?" The pilot jerked our tiny plane higher and higher to avoid an oncoming aircraft. "He was NOT supposed to be there!" he yelled again before dialing in on the radio. Angry and stressed, he told the operator what had happened and descended the plane to its normal flight path.

"Damn idiots," he said after hanging up. "We're lucky we had clear conditions today, folks," he spoke into his headset. "That could have been a disaster."

SEPTEMBER 20, 2018

San Juan Island, Washington

We spent the last week wrapping up exploring Alaska and spending more time in Seattle, a city that was starting to grow on me despite my resistance to any type of society at this point.

Last night we set up camp on San Juan Island, one of the main islands in a cluster of islands between Seattle and Vancouver Island, British Columbia, Canada.

The San Juan Islands are known for orca whale viewing, either from kayak, boat, air, or viewing decks on the island. I was determined to get a better look at my favorite animal, knowing this was the place and time to do it. I scheduled a kayak tour and a raft tour during our time here, knowing I wouldn't leave the island without the experience I'd waited so long for.

We got some breakfast sandwiches from a small counter in downtown Friday Harbor and drove to the kayak outfitter. This was my first time kayaking at all, let alone sea kayaking, and I wondered if my upper body strength would be enough to paddle through ocean waves and navigate to the lighthouse where we were stopping for lunch.

After a short demonstration, we were in our kayaks and ready to go. The water was calm and peaceful, and we passed river otters, sea lions, porpoises, bald eagles, deer, and seals on our way out of the harbor.

We were approaching the lighthouse and tasting the floating bull kelp when someone on the cliff above yelled out, "ORCAS!"

The butterflies came back, and I felt alive, with tears welling up in my eyes at the thought of sharing the ocean with these beautiful animals. I looked over my shoulder and was eye level with a few black fins, far enough away to respect their distance but close enough to imagine jumping in and becoming one of them.

I thought about how easy it would be to change my life completely, how exciting it would be to become the most fierce but well-loved predator of the sea. I could swim around all day in a world completely different than my own. I wanted it so bad, but I stayed in the kayak, watching the orca pod glide effortlessly along the top of the calm ocean, secretly wishing they'd come swim up under us and tip the boat over.

After some time in the water, we took a break at the lighthouse, which had a phone you could use to listen to the whales below the water.

The pod was still hanging around while we ate our lunch on the side of the cliff next to the looming lighthouse. I felt so full and so empty at once, but this was progress, and it was more than I'd felt in ten long months.

It was raining when we got back to camp. Our site was half flooded, but our tent was dry. I crawled into my sleeping bag in the middle of the day and fell asleep to the sound of fat raindrops bouncing off the tent.

SEPTEMBER 21, 2018

I opened my eyes, and my arms were on fire. I felt like I'd lifted weights twice my size for hours on end, tearing every muscle in my arms. I knew my arms would be sore from the ocean kayaking yesterday, but I wasn't prepared for the lack of mobility I had.

Running on the high from kayaking, I was looking forward to the raft whale-watching tour anyway. I'd been on some whale-watching boats, but none were ever specific to orcas. This was my last chance with them before we moved south down the West Coast.

We drove into town and browsed the shops before our tour. I bought my magnet and a glass pipe that looked like Icicle back home. We stopped at a small restaurant called Cynthia's for breakfast and ate on a cute patio with lots of flowers, plants, and herbs. I was really looking forward to seeing the whales. They gave me something to focus on other than Wayne, and even though I felt guilty, it was nice to have something else occupy my mind.

We didn't see any orcas on our whale-watching trip, but we did see a humpback breeching and other wildlife.

I decided we would stay another night to try again the next day. I wasn't going to leave without seeing the orcas.

We got back to camp and tried to heat up a frozen pizza we'd bought at the general store on a piece of aluminum foil over our campfire. After cooking, the crust was completely black, and the toppings were cold and half frozen. I picked at my both overcooked and undercooked dinner, missing Wayne more than ever. I'd grown used to having good luck and giving Wayne credit for aligning the stars for me to have these experiences. I wondered why he was absent when he knew how important it was to me to see the orcas.

I began thinking about what I'd been doing since Wayne's death. The truth is, I'd put Wayne up on a pedestal after he died, like most people do with their dead loved ones. I felt invincible, using Wayne as an excuse to do risky things and justify that I'd be fine because he was watching out for me and wouldn't let anything bad happen to me. This had worked so far, but deep down I wondered how long I could keep going before something terrible happened. *Will I blame him for that too?* I wondered.

I got up and walked across the bright green, manicured lawn to the creek beside my small tent. I pulled a pre-rolled joint from my pocket and tried to light it three times before moving out of the wind. We'd stocked up on weed in Seattle, replenishing what we lost in Wyoming. They had cheap prices and laid-back attitudes, different from the judgment we'd seen back in the Midwest.

I exhaled a long, full breath and stared out across the creek. The rushing water almost drowned out my thoughts and coughs, but not quite. Wayne would have loved Washington. *What would it have been like, sharing these moments with him?* He'd made things so special, exuding genuine excitement and appreciation for whatever we did. I never felt like I had to change myself to impress him or go out of my way to make him love me. We'd had our differences, like anyone, and we worked through more things than we left unfinished.

But the unfinished things didn't stop eating away at me.

He wasn't happy at his last job, something he took in desperation to pay his bills after being let go from Brookfield Zoo. He entered prices into Excel spreadsheets all day for Sears Corporate, and his brilliant mind wasn't being challenged or valued. His expensive environmental biology degree went unused as his student loans piled up. Eventually, he became depressed and fell into an unhealthy routine of staying up all night drinking craft beer and playing video games until 4 a.m., going into work in the afternoon, staying until 8 p.m., and repeating it again the next day.

He'd felt unfulfilled and unhappy when he died, and that guilt weighed heavily on my shoulders. It wasn't the first time he'd fallen into a rut, and I'd once again felt the pressure of covering entire rent payments and living paycheck to paycheck despite my average marketing salary. We'd gotten through worse over ten years, but his hopelessness about his career and student loan debt bled into other aspects of our relationship, and I wasn't as empathetic as I should have been.

My heart skipped a beat, and I started sweating as I thought back to that afternoon in the dark, silent room. Once I tore the curtains open and the bright beam of light flooded the bed, my very first thought while I gazed at my husband's corpse was how relieved he probably felt that he no longer owed sixty thousand dollars on a ten-dollar-an-hour paycheck.

I never told a soul that was where my head went first, before finally blurting it out to a therapist unprovoked. I didn't know what was wrong with me. *Why, out of all our loving memories and things to run through my mind—why was that it? And why couldn't I get into the bed? Why was I so terrified that I waited for the paramedics outside the room, leaving him alone once again?*

I stared into her eyes, waiting for her to tell me I'm a terrible person or get up and leave, disgusted.

"What I hear you saying, Cyndi, is his concerns became your concerns."

I absorbed her perspective, wanting it so badly to be true, needing to prove I wasn't a terrible wife who let her husband die from something so stupid and preventable that it only kills 420 people per year in the United States.

"Your brain was not able to process feelings of grief, because the shock took over," she continued. "You automatically defaulted to something real, something tangible, and something Wayne worried about constantly. You tried to connect any type of relief or explanation for why his death made sense."

Her eyes met mine.

"You were a wonderful wife."

SEPTEMBER 22, 2018

Deception Pass, Washington

It was 11 a.m. when we checked in for the whale tour, and the receptionist, knowing me by now, told us the bad news.

"They're just nowhere to be found," she said apologetically. "You can reschedule for later; things can change fast. You never know."

We rescheduled for later, my confidence dipping by the minute. I found a farmer's market with a little booth that sold homemade cheesecake, the perfect thing to cheer me up while we waited for the last tour of the day.

Time went fast, and we were back in the office. Still no reports of orcas, but the tour was going out anyway. Might as well try one more time.

We loaded into the boat, a tiny vessel with floor to ceiling windows and a huge rubber bumper all around the bottom, reminding me of bumper boats at a carnival. About a half-hour into the ride, a call came through the captain's radio confirming a transient orca pod outside of the tour's usual boundaries.

Normally, the southern resident orcas are seen around the islands, a few playful pods that hunt Chinook salmon and are sometimes friendly and curious with nearby humans. The transients hunt seals and other large mammals, are more aloof, and live alone or in pods with fewer than ten whales.

The captain turned to everyone on the boat, asking if we had anywhere to be later.

"It might be a late night!" he exclaimed. I felt that feeling again, the excitement I'd lost that only seemed to come back for orca whales. Perhaps they reminded me of simpler times when I was a child and had less worry and more energy to fantasize.

We turned around and went the opposite way we were headed, speeding out into the open ocean in search of the transient pod. We passed under Deception Pass Bridge, two large bridges that connect Whidbey Island and Fidalgo Island. Deception Pass is Puget Sound's most narrow passage, a scenic place where tides rush through two channels between cliffs and islands full of salmon, sea lions, and whales, blocking storm swells and tsunamis from the Pacific Ocean.

According to legend, Captain Cook named this passage in 1792. This dangerous area is a prime destination for fishermen, kayakers, photographers, and tourists. If the tide is going out— flowing west—and a strong wind or storm blows from the Pacific, enormous waves become ship-sinking beasts.

I was grateful for the beautiful day, with no storms in sight.

Our captain told us stories about boats that would get caught up in storms while people on the bridge watched helplessly. When the storms end, divers don't search for corpses because of deep currents that carry the dead away. If someone goes missing, Coast Guard helicopters fly search patterns, and rescue boats scan for bodies. Bodies without life jackets are usually never seen again, though remains are sometimes found. They can wash ashore miles away, days later.

I shoved my hand into my pocket and squeezed the plastic

tube. At least Wayne's body was with me, as much as it could be. I was grateful he wasn't lost at sea.

We left the pass behind and sailed out even further, getting close to where the orcas had been spotted. Not too long after, I heard the unmistakable sound of a blowhole, followed by a couple more.

This time, I had a front-row seat. There were three orcas, one clearly a calf. Their sleek backs and long dorsal fins sparkled in the sun, with a rainbow appearing above when they surfaced.

They weren't at all concerned by our presence, or if they were, they didn't show it because the determination in their body language couldn't be more apparent. They were hunting a seal.

They ran it in circles, over and over and over until it got tired and slowed down. Our boat sat in the same place, all the passengers in awe, witnessing something firsthand that's only seen on the Discovery Channel.

Even when the seal slowed, the orcas chased, probably teaching the calf how to hunt. They could have eaten the seal for dinner by now, but the poor thing was still being teased and pursued.

I watched silently, thanking Wayne in my head. I knew he was behind this.

The orcas disappeared under the surface, hiding their secrets from us. A few seconds later, the seal came shooting out of the water with the power of a canon, flipping through the air before smacking back on the surface several hundred feet from where it began.

The orcas were tossing it around like a ragdoll. Exhausted, the seal gave up, not moving or fighting anymore.

I understood, but I wanted him to get up and swim away to safety. I wanted him to try harder. Was I a hypocrite? Part of me also envied the seal; giving up seemed so much easier.

The orcas started thrashing as the seagulls and seabirds above congregated on top of the scene, waiting for the leftovers.

We watched the scene unfold for about an hour, then turned back. The sun was setting, and the water started getting choppier by the minute.

We were miles and miles away from Friday Harbor, and I could sense the crew's body language begin to change. The mood switched from fun and lighthearted to quiet and stoic while they made sure everyone was off the outer decks and inside the boat.

The waves picked up and grew twice as big almost immediately, with no warning. Our boat was rocking back and forth like a hollow stick in a raging river. The decks filled with water as the wave walls towered over the top and splashed into the boat.

The crew started gathering life jackets and told us to stay calm and seated. I glanced over at the woman next to me as her whimpers became louder, pulling me out of my shock and into reality.

"We have some real bad weather coming in," the captain breathed through the loudspeaker. "Please hold on."

I looked over at Shaun, not really having anything to say but wanting to break the loud silence that lingered after the announcement. It's always the silence. He stared straight ahead.

There were about ten other people on the boat, and the only sound I heard was the roaring of the waves overtaking us. Some passengers were clinging to the seats in front of them; others were holding their loved ones tightly.

I gazed outside, barely making out a mix of gray sky and black ocean through the raindrop-soaked glass.

The captain clung to the steering wheel, his white knuckles like blinding spotlights.

I felt like the seal, helplessly tossed into the air and smashed back down with a force that took my breath away. It was my turn to give up.

I didn't feel much, at least not how you think you'd react right before your boat sinks into the Pacific Ocean. I thought about Wayne and how happy he'd be to see me, and I felt good about dying after seeing something so rare and natural. It made sense. It was worth it.

The boat dipped below the waterline with a swell, and a wall of icy water smashed through the floor-to-ceiling windows, bursting open the door that led out to the front and hitting us in the face with a force of one hundred right hooks.

Water was pouring through the cracks in the windows, and the woman next to me started to hyperventilate. She was alone, and I wondered about her family.

I wondered about mine too. I wanted to call my parents, but I had no service. I thought about what I would say to them if I had the chance, like how I'd thought about what I would have said to Wayne if I'd known it was the last time I was going to see him.

I certainly wouldn't have talked about getting gas before work because I was on empty or how jealous I was of his weight loss from being sick after our honeymoon.

Instead I would have told him all the things I loved about him, down to every last detail. The way I fit perfectly in his shoulder and how we called it "the spot." The way he loved his family. His witty but humble humor. His confidence in who he was and his vulnerability to showing his emotions. The way he listened to me and supported everything I did.

A few inches of water flooded the floor. I lifted my feet up despite being soaked from head to toe already. I put on my life jacket and remembered we shouldn't even be on this tour. This was my third time in two days attempting to see the orcas, and we should have just left after the first time. The crew was so great in letting us reschedule and went out of their way to find the orcas, because they knew how important it was to me after learning why I was here.

I felt responsible. *I'm going to kill all these people. People who have families and children and husbands and wives and jobs and purposes and the will to live.* We were still navigating through the angry waters, slowly but surely, our captain mentioning we might reroute to Anacortes for the night.

I held Shaun's hand and looked over his way. His sleek, straight black hair covered his closed almond-shaped eyes as it was matted down with salt water that dripped onto his black framed glasses. I wondered what he was thinking about, or if he felt guilty the way I did.

Despite our arguments, I'd grown to love Shaun in a way I'd never loved another person before. What we had was deeper than a friendship, closer than any family relationship, and uniquely intimate but not romantic.

He had learned a lot about me in the months following Wayne's death. He'd folded my underwear, slept on my couch, spent time with my family, and listened to me grieve and talk about Wayne for hours.

He'd talked about his strict childhood and broken family dynamic, and we'd supported each other through the loss. Nobody understood me like Shaun. I was the most vulnerable I'd ever been, and not even Wayne had seen me this low. Shaun's support was overwhelming, often making me question what I did to deserve his help.

"You're Wayne's wife," he would say. "I know he'd do it for me."

Somehow, we managed to make it back to Friday Harbor a couple of hours later, thanks to the careful maneuvering of our captain.

"We just replaced our old boats with these a few months ago," he said before we disembarked. "These are Coast Guard-certified. If we were caught out there without 'em, we woulda sunk."

We got back to the marina in time to catch the last ferry back to Seattle after a short and silent walk through town to grab my car. We both knew it was a close call, and there just wasn't much to say.

SEPTEMBER 29, 2018

Olympic National Park, Washington

We spent the last seven days exploring Olympic National Park and hiding in the tent. I didn't want to leave the luxury of the blow-up mattress we would set up in our eight-person fortress for long stays. It felt like a mansion—with room to stand, a place for our clothes bags, a queen-size bed to stretch out on, and even a rug by the front door. This was the closest thing to a real home I'd had in months, and it felt good to stay in one place for longer than a day or two.

Olympic National Park is huge and diverse, boasting snowcapped mountains; seventy miles of rugged coastal beaches with sea stacks and tide pools full of starfish, urchins, fish, crabs, and sea otters; old growth trees in the Hoh Rainforest; and countless waterfalls, lakes, and rivers.

We spent long nights on the beaches, watching the sun set into the stars to display brilliantly dark skies under the bright shine of the Milky Way.

My favorite beach, identified by a number and not a proper name, was wild and deserted. Endless steps descended through a moss-covered forest with a fast-flowing creek to the left. At the bottom of the stairs, the forest opened to a wooden bridge made of the beach's driftwood. The creek flowing underneath spilled out to the right side, creating a waterfall down the rock formations which disappeared into the soft sand, eventually emptying into the open ocean. A raggedy but sturdy rope tied to the bridge helped us shimmy down the smooth, slippery stone to the beach, which had tide pools to the north and south that brimmed with sea life during low tide.

I grabbed the rope, happy to be at my new favorite spot. Wayne and I had gotten married one year ago today, and the anticipation of the pain leading up to our anniversary overtook me with paralyzing anxiety and depression on the days prior.

I hadn't left the tent or even drank water for two days, smoking myself into a zombie-like state so I would fall in and out of sleep and not feel anything. The hours passed by quickly, despite my inactivity. I reverted to the early days, eating peanut butter from the jar for all my meals, ignoring the rules about food in tents in bear country. Even boiling water in my electric tea kettle for freeze-dried meals felt too overwhelming.

I let go of the rope and jumped down the last few feet to the beach. Sunrays exploded through the monstrous trees from above, filtering through the fine morning mist and creating a spotlight on the violent ocean.

The waves of the Pacific crashed onto towering sea stacks scattered throughout the water, which were home to different species during low tide. The salt and mist clung to my skin, absorbing all of me.

The uprooted, fallen driftwood was stacked and thrown haphazardly atop one another by strong storms, and it lined the rocky shorelines for miles. The bleached and bare trees, destroyed by the fierce ocean winds, appeared ghostly against the dark sand, smooth to the touch from years of erosion.

I sat down on a massive piece of driftwood with the entire length of its tree and root system preserved. I gazed at the mixture of dead western red cedar, Sitka spruce, Douglas fir, bigleaf maple, and western hemlock trees—amazed at the power of nature—while Shaun studied rocks.

We'd spent days swallowed up in the old-growth forests of Washington, trekking beneath hundred-year-old trees and feeling their majestic energy. There, they felt so strong, so in charge. Giants of the forest, protecting everything else below them.

Here, the trees formed a graveyard. A memorial of what once stood healthy and towering.

I looked out at the open ocean, mesmerized at the foamy water and crab leg remnants.

We hadn't gotten Wayne a headstone. It hung heavy on my shoulders like an overstuffed hiking bag, but not because I thought it was important. In 1990, his grandparents had buried their son, Wayne's dad, in the cemetery across from where the funeral was held. They bought two extra plots next door to complete the family graveyard when it was time.

For Wayne's dad, they'd had an industry-leading headstone made with an engraved photo of him on the front, a brand-new option back then. There was even a story about it in the local newspaper.

The family wanted the same for Wayne, and his grandpa gave up his plot for his grandson who ended up dying first. He wanted to be buried in the veteran memorial cemetery anyway, he said.

Wayne and I were too young and naive to talk seriously about death, but I knew enough to know he wanted to be cremated. I didn't see the point of a grave for his ashes; I wanted them with me. Thinking about Wayne alone inside the ground in any capacity made my stomach churn. He still deserved to be a part of our lives.

He was with me now, and I was leaving parts of him in the most beautiful places around our country that he never got to see. One of Wayne's aunts—the same one who refused to come to our wedding because we made it adults-only, and the same one who called me a crazy cannibal when she found out I'd sprinkled some ashes on pizza like parmesan cheese—said these places meant nothing to Wayne, and I shouldn't have control of the decisions.

I know there's nowhere he'd rather be than with me—exploring, loving, laughing, and learning.

I had been dreading today and this time of year for months, knowing it would set off a domino effect of grief that I may or may not be able to control. *Wedding. Honeymoon. Death. Wedding. Honeymoon. Death. Wedding honeymoon death wedding honeymoondeath weddingmoon. Moondeath. Death. Death.*

I wondered what we'd be doing today for our one-year anniversary. We already ate the top of the wedding cake a few days after the wedding, standing in the kitchen with the fridge door open, forks intertwined and giggling like children. It was marble flavored with a homemade cream cheese frosting, adorned with burlap flowers running down the side and a black metal cake topper with cats. We didn't want to freeze the cake for an entire year.

"It will be dry," Wayne reasoned. "It's so good now." It was gone within a couple of days, disappearing quickly since we ate a bite or two (or three) every time we opened the fridge.

Our wedding had been quaint and beautiful, a literal fairytale with the most tragic ending. It was a crisp, fall day with a deep blue sky and billowy passing clouds. Our ceremony took place in a tiny garden with autumn-colored mums and other flowers under an arch with golden leaves. We wrote our own vows and felt like the only two people around when reading them to each other.

Small waterfalls dotted the cobblestone paths, and fish swam through ponds next to fireplaces with wooden benches. When it got dark, the gardens and trees lit up with fairy lights of all different colors, and fires roared, roasting late night s'mores.

We paid special attention to the food and menu, serving acorn squash soup with an assortment of freshly baked breads and filet mignon with roasted vegetables and garlic mashed potatoes. Wayne made the music playlists, separating out the ceremony, cocktail hour, and dinner lists with songs from our past. I made the centerpieces with dried flowers and dead branches from our campground, wrapped in twinkling lights in tall vases.

We danced and visited with family and took photos in the shadows of the soft amber glow. It was warm, it was us, it was perfect. For weeks after, Wayne couldn't stop telling me it truly was the best day of his life.

We spent a long time taking photos alone in the shadows of the soft amber glow that night. I felt like we were missing too much of the ceremony, and I wanted to go back to join our friends and family.

"We'll want these to look back on and remember," he said. "Try not to rush things, and enjoy the moment."

Now, all I have are the photos to remind me, I thought as I reflected back. Because as much as I'd love to look back and remember this day and all the details organically, a lot of it got lost in the grief that came just six weeks later.

My wedding photos, for me, almost served as proof that it really happened. That this was my life at one point, because it often felt like a dream that never came true.

OCTOBER 1, 2018

Mount Rainier National Park, Washington

The last couple of days were rainy and foggy, obstructing our view of Mount Rainier, the third tallest singular peak in the US. Ascending over 14,000 feet above sea level, the active volcano is the most glaciated peak in the contiguous US and has five major rivers, but it hasn't erupted since the 1800s.

On days with high visibility, the mountain towers over Seattle and the surrounding area, causing locals to exclaim, "The mountain is out!" This brings particular joy during long winter seasons when she hardly shows herself.

In the summer, the highest peaks stand covered in snow well into August, and the clear, warm weather displays her grandiosity nearly every day. The Wonderland Trail, a ninety-three-mile loop trail that encircles the mountain, is difficult but rewarding, with constant inclines and declines from the volcano's ridges, rock and snow fields, nooks, crannies, and river valleys. Even if the weather is good, the underbrush and shoulder-height foliage soak adventurers every morning, but the unpredictable terrain provides breathtaking views, scenic camps, abundant fresh water, and a life-changing experience.

While we weren't braving the Wonderland Trail, we drove and hiked to several waterfalls, each unique in its own way. We explored "Paradise," the part of the park opposite "Sunrise." Canadian whiskey jays landed on our outstretched hands and shoulders, hoping to get a treat. And while the mountain was hiding the whole time we were there, the forests and meadows at the base exploded with bright autumn foliage, partially hidden by a thick layer of gray fog that made the vivid pops of color stand out even more. We counted five black bears in one day, and I vowed to come back and get a better view of the mountain in the future.

We were headed to Portland, Oregon, to spend a couple of days exploring the city before camping in Crater Lake National Park. As much as I'd fought Shaun about stopping in the cities, I began cherishing and looking forward to the welcome breaks that included hot showers, real food, and somewhere else to sit other than a car seat or picnic table in the woods.

In two days, we devoured biscuit breakfast sandwiches, Voodoo Doughnuts and Blue Star Donuts, Salt & Straw Ice Cream, Pok Pok chicken wings, Tillamook cheese and ice cream, handmade pasta from a food cart, and several different versions of Oregon's official state dish, marionberry pie, before driving the four short hours to Crater Lake.

OCTOBER 4, 2018

Crater Lake National Park, Oregon

Being that it was shoulder season, we felt like the only ones on Earth as we got closer to Crater Lake's gate. We'd been driving for hours, and the darkness engulfed everything around us, blinding me to the forest and any other landmarks we may have passed.

I looked out the window and up at the sky. It was a cold, crisp, clear night, and the stars appeared closer than I'd ever seen.

"Stop the car," I said. "You have to see this."

He pulled over, and we both got out of the car, our visible breath bursting through the cold night air. There was nothing around us except endless lines of trees and billions of twinkling stars above. I could barely see Shaun in front of me, even though I could hear his chilled, shallow breaths.

The Big and Little Dipper, Orion's Belt, and other constellations—along with The Milky Way—appeared so close it felt like I could reach out and pluck them from the sky. They flashed so brightly; they looked like diamonds against a black velvet background every time I moved my head. Crater Lake is listed by the National Park Service's Dark Sky Team as one of the top ten dark sky locations in the US, with little to no light pollution at a higher elevation and only a small population of local tribes.

It was hard to leave, but somehow, I pulled myself away from the diamonds in the sky. We had to find and set up camp in the pitch dark, one of my least favorite things that almost always seemed to happen.

We found a free campground by a rushing river with a small, overflowing outhouse. All the sites were empty, and the river roared so loud we had to shout to hear each other. I grabbed the tiny tent from the back of the car and clipped the nylon fabric onto the poles, getting it upright in seconds.

I found a rock in the woods nearby, hammered the tent stakes into the soft ground, and covered the structure with the rainfly. It was supposed to rain overnight despite the clear sparkling skies, and I'd learned not to repeat the first night back in the Badlands.

I walked to the wooden outhouse a few hundred feet east of our campsite, thankful to have somewhere to go other than the woods but almost preferring the clean solitude the trees gave over the nose-piercing smell of an overflowing hole full of shit. I put my jacket up over my nose, but that only made it worse with direct access from the ground to my nostrils.

I'd learned how to do what I needed to do more efficiently than ever before, and I was out in a matter of minutes, running from the seat and letting the heavy wooden door slam behind me. Fresh air had never smelled so sweet.

We ate dark chocolate peanut butter granola bars and tiny tangerines for dinner, not wanting to mess with anything extravagant in the dark, and passed out from lack of things to do.

I woke up several hours later, having felt like I slept an entire night, but it was still pitch black outside the tent. I shifted to my back and lay awake, listening to the rain bounce off the roof, letting my eyes adjust to the dim, filtered moonlight. I had to pee so bad, but the warmth of my sleeping bag and the thought of walking to the shitty hole in the ground in the rain held me hostage.

I sat up in my sleeping bag and searched for my weed. I'd fallen asleep with it in my hand, and it was lost in the abyss underneath me. It was always within reach during the night, a habit I'd created when I would go to sleep crying and wake up in the middle of the night from the shock and immediate disappointment of seeing Wayne alive in my dreams, knowing it wasn't real and it never would be. Weed abolished my nightmares and gave me back the precious gift of sleep, even if I did have to wake up at 3 a.m. and take another hit to remain unconscious for a few more hours.

I found the disposable vape with my foot and rolled it up along my right side slowly, so I wouldn't wake Shaun with my rustles of desperation. I brought it to my lips and took a bigger drag than I meant to, erupting in a fit of uncontrollable coughs and gasps for air. He opened his eyes and looked at me, half amused and half annoyed. He held out his hand, and I gave him the pen. He smoked and handed it back.

"What time is it?" he asked, rolling over in his sleeping bag to face me.

"I don't even know," I answered. "I didn't want to look. I can't sleep."

"Only midnight?!" he exclaimed into the brightness of his phone. "Fuck."

I sighed and climbed out of my sleeping bag. There was no way I could hold my pee for another six or seven hours.

"Don't you have your Go-Girl?" he asked with a half-smile. I laughed louder than I should have, piercing through and drowning out the river. I did have it with me, tucked away unused in a Ziplock in my necessities bag under my pillow.

I reached under my head and grabbed the cloth drawstring bag. I pulled out the fake purple penis, a silicone vessel you're supposed to be able to press against your pelvis so you can piss like a man whenever you want, wherever you want. I hadn't had the balls to try it—clearly, we'd been on the road for two months already, and it was still rolled up like a foreskin, waiting to be unraveled. It seemed like a good idea, so I opened the bag, and it flopped open and bounced onto my lap.

I made eye contact with Shaun and unzipped my side of the tent. I rolled my leggings down to my knees and held up my sleeping bag for a makeshift stall, not breaking our stare.

"Don't look!" I hissed, laughing but entirely serious. "Turn around!"

I held the flat silicone funnel flush to my body and got as close to the edge of the tent as I could. The spout was facing far enough outside that I was confident my stream would be strong enough to run down with the rain.

"So?" he questioned me, laughing but curious about my progress.

"I'm trying!" I whisper-yelled as he unzipped his side of the tent.

"This is how it's done," he beamed, finishing up before I even started.

Frustrated, I closed my eyes and blocked everything out except the sound of the rainwater hitting the ground. I'd been standing there for minutes now, the urge to pee seemingly disappearing while the fear of soiling my sleeping area took over. I concentrated and let myself relax. Finally, I felt it.

I felt it down my thigh and leg while also watching a weak stream pour out the tip, barely making it out of the tent door.

"Damnit!" I screamed, tightening my muscles mid-stream and jumping out into the rain—the very thing I was trying to avoid.

His hysterical laughter intertwined with mine as I took my pants and underwear off and hopped around on one foot in the dark, wet woods. I squatted behind a tree, rinsed my legs and disaster dick, and finished peeing like a lady before retreating to my car for some clean clothes.

OCTOBER 7, 2018

Crater Lake National Park, Oregon

It was our last day at Crater Lake, a sunny, brilliantly blue day that made the deepest lake in the US (seventh in the world) a deeper blue than I'd ever seen in nature. Crater Lake is almost two thousand feet deep and was formed when Mount Mazama, a twelve-thousand-foot-tall volcano, erupted and collapsed about eight thousand years ago. It left behind a large, empty crater in the earth that slowly filled with pristine mountain snow and rain—leaving no sediment or mineral deposits. This, and the fact that there are no inlets to allow other water sources to flow through, is why it's so clear.

We'd explored the park's Rim Road in the days before, a thirty-three-mile road that spit us out at countless scenic pullouts and left us marveling at frozen volcanic ash shaped into one-hundred-foot rock formations. The park boasts ponderosa pines, lodgepole pines, whitebark pines, and mountain hemlocks, creating a stroke of green to counter the dominating deep blue.

We'd had enough of the view from the rim and wanted to touch the water on our last day. It was too cold to swim, but I wanted to at least soak my feet and leave Wayne's ashes in one of the cleanest lakes in the world. Cleetwood Cove Trail has the only legal access to the shore of Crater Lake and is usually only open from mid-June to late October. At just over two miles roundtrip, this short but steep hike can be strenuous, dropping seven hundred feet of elevation over one mile through a series of long switchbacks.

The trail surface is crushed pumice, loose and slippery when conditions are dry. Hiking back up the trail is comparable to climbing sixty-five flights of stairs. With the high elevation, air temperature, and airborne trail-dust and smoke from local wildfires (which is common during the dry summers), conditions can be dangerous. Most of search and rescue operations in Crater Lake stem from hikers being unable to ascend the trail once they have hiked down to the lakeshore. In the summer, the average surface temperature of the lake is only fifty-seven degrees Fahrenheit, chilly enough to get you out of the water after only a cliff jump or two on even the hottest days.

I was confident enough by now that I'd be able to complete the hike without even stopping at one of the various benches generously placed on the switchbacks for resting. With two months of consistent hiking and a lack of real food for most of it, I'd lost even more weight, and my legs and calves were hardening by the day with newly developed muscle.

The walk down was quick and easy for someone with no knee problems. The morning was warming, and the October sun began to burn my still-pale-but-tanning skin. The calm, sapphire water sparkled under the light, and I wished I'd remembered my sunglasses. I felt like I could see through to the bottom of the lake from what seemed like miles above it; the shore started clear, then turned into a teal green before blending a lighter blue into a darker blue the further out I looked. Large boulders and rocks lined the bottom of the lake and the shore around it, providing plenty of privacy for anyone around to enjoy the view in solitude.

I found a spot on the edge of some flat boulders and looked west, directly out to Wizard Island, a volcanic cinder cone that formed an island in the lake—basically, a volcano inside of a volcano. The top of Wizard Island reaches almost 7,000 feet above sea level, about 755 feet above the average surface of the lake. In the summer, they offer boat tours to the island where you can camp overnight.

Pictures didn't do it justice. They didn't do any of what I saw justice, just as these words can't possibly explain the wild beauty and healing powers of nature.

I peeled off my sweaty socks and dusty trail runners and pulled my purple leggings above my knees. The sun was hot but the breeze was cold, and it felt glorious on my bare, tired feet. I dipped my toes in first, measuring the water's temperature before I submerged my legs. The shock of the cold wore off quickly after I realized, *My body is inside one of America's most pure assets*. The tiny inland waves washed up over my feet and ankles, now red from the freezing water.

I leaned against an adjacent rock that formed a natural backrest behind me, and I closed my eyes. A wave of gratitude washed over me with the small waves at my feet. I was sitting in an almost eight-thousand-year-old crater, washing my dirty, smelly feet in thousand-year-old rain and snowmelt. Hard rock wall, endless evergreens, and treacherous cliffsides rose hundreds of feet above me, and while impressive, they didn't hold a candle to the wonders almost two thousand feet below.

While there's no evidence native fish ever lived in Crater Lake, humans stocked it with seven different species of fish between 1888 and 1941, and only two are left: about sixty thousand kokanee salmon and rainbow trout. Deep tubes, pits, holes, and depressions called *fumaroles* start on the surface of thousand-year-old dead moss layers on the bottom of the lake, extending up to sixteen feet into the ground.

I grabbed the blue joint tube and dumped a portion of Wayne's ashes into the lake. They sparkled like glitter, moving through the water gracefully in a cloud before dissolving before my eyes. He was there, and then he was gone. It happened over and over and over, every time I scattered his ashes, every time I thought about him, every time I closed my eyes. He was there, and then he was gone.

After a couple of hours at the lake, we made the trek back up seven hundred feet of elevation in one mile, easily passing by exhausted visitors and comfortable-looking wooden benches. There was a certain power in grief I hadn't recognized before. A power in myself I never knew existed. I could do anything. Nothing scared me. Nothing intimated me.

It was four hours west to Redwood National Park in northern California. Halfway through, we stopped at my first ever In-N-Out Burger. Which, to be honest, was anything but in and out. We sat in the drive-through near Grants Pass, Oregon, for over an hour and a half, the line weaving around the parking lot and onto the street. I didn't care. We lit a joint and rolled down our windows, playing one of Wayne's playlists from 2016 while we waited. Finally, we were eating four double doubles, animal style, parked in a dark spot in the back of the parking lot. It was exactly what I needed.

OCTOBER 19, 2018

Yosemite National Park, California

We spent the last couple of weeks traversing Redwood National and State Parks and driving down the 101, covering the entirety of northern and central California. We took days hiking coastal beach trails filled with bright yellow banana slugs the length of my middle fingers and trudging upstream in Fern Canyon, a filming location for *The Lost World: Jurassic Park*. The narrow, green canyon is engulfed by fifty-foot rock walls exploding with oversized ferns. Fresh waterfalls trickle down from the top through textured mosses, and a creek fills the inside of the canyon over a rocky bottom. Massive, downed redwood trees create height and places to climb while wild mushrooms dot the canyon walls and ground, fighting for any filtered sunlight that makes it through the thick canopy of trees and ferns.

I didn't want to leave the unbelievable trees and salty coast behind. The massive trunks and sprawling height reminded me of Wayne, our *Tree*, and I felt at home among the redwoods. Their stationary security made me feel safe, like when Wayne towered over everyone else in a crowd and I knew he'd always be there to shield me from anything.

But we were on our way southeast, with a target of Yosemite National Park, and I looked forward to this stop for more than a few reasons. The route was mountainous, and the air felt chillier by the mile as we drove into the remote national forest land. Endless diverse landscapes blurred by as we took turns driving and sleeping. Eventually, we made it close enough to the park that we were satisfied to stop and rest for the night.

It was pitch black when we pulled up to an abandoned national forest campground, with no facilities or people to speak of. We quickly started our setup routine, and I had the tiny green tent standing in seconds while Shaun shoved all our warmest gear in through the zippered door. We first covered the top of the tent with a large, brown fuzzy blanket, then attached the rainfly. We'd learned that with the extra blanket, and by transforming our own sleeping bags into one big bag that we shared, our body heat kept us much more insulated on nights that dipped below zero. Although it was freezing, we stayed relatively warm in the small space throughout the night, until I awoke in the very early morning hours when the condensation from our restless breath transformed into ice crystals and frost that blanketed both the inside and outside of the tent. It was only 4 a.m., and I shivered my way through until sunrise, noting to stock up on body warmers and rubber water bottles next time we were near a store. Once the first glimpse of soft pink and blue filled the sky, I shook Shaun awake to get the day started. We packed up as quickly as we'd set up, leaving no trace of our presence.

The inconvenience of living in a car was starting to get to me, and I found myself wishing for a home base to call my own, although I tried to push back those feelings as much as possible. A house is not a home without Wayne anyway.

This was going to be a long day, with multiple waterfall hikes to undertake and a fierce competition for open campsites inside the gates, and I'd already felt tired. While it was supposed to be the shoulder season during this time of year for normal visitors, Yosemite in October overflows with rock climbers trying to make the most of the mild weather, jamming the interior campgrounds and increasing the traffic in the park considerably.

It was still early morning when we drove through the gates and into the park for the first time. All my life, I'd heard stories about the grand Half Dome, the tallest waterfall in the US, the beautiful Yosemite Valley, and El Capitan. But nothing prepared me for the vast, magical scenery that greeted us around the bend after the Wawona Tunnel. If I had stepped into an alternate universe when Wayne died, I was stepping into another one now. The scene in front of me could have only been dreamed up from a fantasy world full of goodness and love. Something like this belonged to a different planet, not this Earth bursting with pain and suffering. All the famous scenes of Yosemite were shoved into this one expansive view, like a Bob Ross painting. Every pretty little tree and happy little accident was perfectly placed exactly where it needed to be to create one of the most breathtaking backdrops in the country. The looming gray granite rock walls cradled sparkling waterfalls above a valley of green pine trees and lush meadows, and we drove around the twists and bends in silence.

The Bridalveil Fall Trail was first on our list of waterfall hikes, a quick walk of just under a mile to the base of the towering falls. To get under the 620-foot falls, a moderate rock wall separates the base from the accessible part of the trail, requiring a small amount of scrambling up the smooth, slippery granite. In the parking lot, we hopped out of the car for the falls, and I kept my old, light sneakers on, as this was the shortest and easiest hike of the popular routes, nothing more than a leisurely stroll for my newly formed leg muscles.

The trailhead began at the end of the parking lot, and we reached the slippery boulders quickly. Shaun scrambled up easily, but I slipped on the smooth surface and fell a few feet down a small crevasse into a clear, rushing stream, soaking my shoes in freezing glacial water. I tried to climb my way back up, but my shoes had next to no traction, and the water didn't help. Every time I tried to take a step, I slipped. I stood in the stream and looked up at the rock walls surrounding me. *This is fine,* I thought. *He'll realize I'm no longer with him, and come back looking for me.* I retreated to a tiny shelter under the granite and sat on a wet rock, trying to decide what to do next. I was literally stuck between a rock and a hard place.

Thirty minutes came and went, and I realized he wasn't coming back for me. My heart started to beat a little faster than normal, and my breath became shallower as the minutes ticked by. Every attempt at climbing back up the smooth, vertical rocks failed, and I was getting desperate to escape. The close proximately to the parking lot was almost amusing; I was so close to civilization, yet I felt so far away and forgotten. Nobody on this Earth knew where I was, and that's exactly what I had wanted over the last year. Now that it was really happening, I felt even more lost and alone.

Another thirty minutes passed. *Shaun must have just missed me when he came back looking. He must have walked right above me.* I took off my wet shoes and socks. Maybe I'd be able to get enough traction to boost myself up using my bare feet. *I can do this on my own.* I grabbed onto the tiny notch in the rock I'd been using to lift myself off the ground, and I swung my legs and feet up as far as they would go. I felt the bottoms of my feet grip the granite, and I used all my upper body strength to propel the rest of my body out of the crevasse and onto level ground.

My legs were shaking when I stepped onto the stable pavement, and I was surprised at how unsettled I felt. Feeling any type of emotion other than numb was a step in the right direction, but getting lost on such an easy, quick trail humbled me quickly. I could have broken a bone or hit my head and been trapped between the boulders forever, without ever being discovered. I thought about what it would mean for my family and my cats back home in Illinois. My heart ached at the thought of Icicle and Goose losing both of their humans in a matter of months and not understanding why. I'd left them behind without giving it a second thought; the loss of Wayne had rendered me feelingless. Even the most important parts of my life were no longer important; I'd already lost so much. But I still had them, and the thought of seeing their tiny faces and warm bellies again kept me going. I hoped they knew I was going to come back for them. I promised I would.

After regaining the strength in my legs, I started back the way we came, retracing our steps to find the parking lot. I figured the smartest thing would be to meet at my car, and I hoped Shaun was there waiting to leave. My dark gray SUV came into focus as I neared the lot, and I instantly felt at home. Even though I was getting sick of living in a car with another person, my car was once again my comfort, my lifeline.

I realized I didn't have my keys—Shaun did—so I collapsed onto the curb and looked up at the waterfall, visible and impressive from the parking lot. *Where is he?* I thought there was no way he could still be at the end of the trail waiting for me. *Or is he?* I was about to head back to the trail to search for him when I saw a tall figure heading my way, walking across the parking lot. Relief flooded my body, and we met back up like we'd never left each other, though I still wondered how far he'd gotten before realizing I was missing.

We stopped at the small but well-stocked general store off the park's main road to refuel before hiking the Mist Trail, an appropriate name for the refreshing sprinkle of Sierra Nevada mountain water that creates rainbows on nature's "giant staircase" leading up to a 317-foot waterfall. We found a full, fresh rotisserie chicken, which was unheard of at any other park facilities, so we took the opportunity to get some extra protein in our diets in anticipation of a tough seven-mile hike with four thousand feet of elevation gain.

Shaun stopped at the bathroom while I paid for our chicken and other fixings, and I carried the bag of food outside to one of the picnic tables in front of the store. I took our purchases out one by one and placed the full loaf of bread next to the large, cooked chicken. Complete with a slice of cheddar cheese and some barbeque sauce, our idea for chicken sandwiches was making my mouth water. Usually, we'd be lucky to find beef jerky, hard-boiled eggs, cheese sticks, and ice cream sandwiches at these stores. Yosemite really was grand.

I'd started to assemble the sandwiches when I realized we didn't have our bag of plastic silverware with us, so I didn't have anything to cut the chicken with. Oh well. I opened the plastic container, pulled out one of the breasts, and began to shred it with my fingers. I shredded the second breast and picked up one of the legs before catching the eye of a woman my age, maybe a bit younger, sitting with her friend. They were both watching me sitting alone with my whole chicken and entire bread loaf, shredding the meat, and licking my fingers like a caveman. They laughed and whispered to each other. The disgusted looks on their faces were all I needed to know that they'd been watching and making fun of me the whole time.

I guess I had lost some manners over the course of the road trip; I wasn't used to being in public or around a lot of people, and I wasn't used to caring about things that didn't matter. I had forgotten how judgmental everyone was. Had *they* lost their homes and been living out of a car for the last three months? Did *their* husbands die suddenly? Why did they care what I was doing at all? Suddenly, I'd felt enraged. Surprised at my own reaction, I looked them right in their faces without breaking eye contact. Before Wayne's death, an awkward encounter like this would have sent me in a people pleasing spiral of apologies, justifications, and shame, but now, I felt sorry for them. First, because they weren't going to taste my delicious sandwiches. But mostly because they were assholes.

Shaun sauntered out, interrupting the silent showdown, and we downed our pulled-chicken sandwiches in record time before conquering a half-mile vertical staircase and countless rocky switchbacks.

It was dark by the time we finished our five-hour hike around Vernal and Nevada Falls, and we still hadn't secured a campsite. Exhausted, we climbed into the car and headed down to the campgrounds. I had my head on the passenger's window and was looking out into the black night when a flash of light caught my eye.

Endless twinkling lights filled the night sky, like hundreds of fireflies gathering for a nighty ritual. Half Dome, illuminated by a million shining stars, cast a deep shadow over Yosemite Valley.

I'd later find out the twinkling lights were from the rock climbers' flashlights moving through the night.

NOVEMBER 18, 2018

Death Valley National Park, California

The past month had gone by in a blur, and my memories of last year's honeymoon and death date loomed over me. My body was slower, and I lacked motivation as the days dragged on.

We'd explored Sequoia, King's Canyon, and Pinnacles National Parks, spotting turkey vultures, raccoons, birds, deer, and a tarantula. One cold, pitch-black night, after being too lazy to walk to the bathrooms across the campground, I'd crashed into the numbered site post after trying to back out of the tight spot, putting a large, unmistakable dent in my bumper. I laughed it off, remembering a similar incident in Yellowstone with Wayne all those years ago. But instead of laughing it off then, I was bothered, and I wish I'd known then what I learned later.

We took a short break in Los Angeles where Shaun and I explored the Griffith Observatory; ate the best Tsukemen (ramen dipping noodles) with the richest, most delicious pork broth and chewiest noodles in the States; ate our weight in tacos al pastor; and decided he would stay on the trip for a little longer.

After leaving L.A, I spent a few drugged days crying in a room in someone's garage Airbnb in San Diego. Eventually, I forced myself to get out from under the covers to visit San Diego Zoo and San Diego Zoo Safari Park to celebrate Wayne's life on November 13, his one-year death anniversary. I spread a bit of his ashes on the safari train tour to symbolize his love for animals and time working at zoos in Chicago and Boston.

We crossed our way from San Diego into Joshua Tree National Park where we hiked through the strong desert sun in a forest of Joshua Trees, enormous, odd rock formations, and flowering cacti. We traversed through salt flats and got sunburns in Death Valley National Park before experiencing some of the most memorable sunsets overlooking the sprawling vistas and vast views.

We were on our way from Death Valley to Great Basin National Park with some pit stops in between when I drove a lot of lonely hours down Highway 50. Dubbed America's Loneliest Road by *Life* magazine in 1968, it stretched between Fernley and Baker, Nevada, and was nothing but straight, open road with almost nothing to look at. *American's loneliest road, America's loneliest girl,* I thought.

Being in Death Valley for several days so close to Wayne's death anniversary really got me thinking a lot about death. That I may not be here in five minutes. Five days. Five weeks. Five months. Five years. I'd never been more aware of my own mortality. *What am I doing with my life?*

Even back in 2015, as Wayne and I sat in a packed room for a past coworker and acquaintance from college who died in a car accident at age twenty-seven, I still didn't grasp the randomness and finality of death. I had watched his young girlfriend, shocked and stunned with tears streaming down her face, and my heart was shredded. I put my hand on Wayne's leg and my head on his shoulder. In that moment, I was so grateful we were both alive and healthy.

But I still never came face to face with my mortality. After that funeral in 2015, I didn't change the things I didn't like about my life. *Because death happens to other people*, I thought. *I have time.* As sad and naive as it was, death was foreign to me. This didn't happen to *my* family; it happened to *other* people. Not me. I was heartbroken for this person, his girlfriend, and his family. But eventually, my life went back to normal, and soon I was only thinking of him on anniversaries and when we had mutual Facebook memories.

That's what happens when we're not close to death. Everyone's lives go back to normal, except for those who are closest to the dead. Those few become lost in a world of people who have put the death behind them. The grieving are left raw, broken, and desperate for any type of relief they can get. A year passes. All the important "firsts" go by. Your loved ones assume you should be doing better by now, but in reality, the growing absence gets harder to deal with. That's when other people start to drift away.

It wasn't until now that I realized I wasted an opportunity to live my life differently with Wayne after our friend died. Two years later, it was me at Wayne's funeral. No second chances. No redoes. No begging, bargaining, or wishful thinking would bring him back to me. I knew I couldn't keep running from the opportunity to change.

"We should put each other down as our beneficiaries." Shaun broke the silence and monotony of the loneliest road—and my screaming, ruminating thoughts about death. *How did he know I was thinking about death?*

"Uh, no." I laughed nervously. "That's weird."

Silence returned, and I continued the drive to Great Basin National Park where we explored Lehman Caves, a series of marble rock passageways filled with stalactites, stalagmites, and other formations. Our tour guide taught us about the bats, millipedes and other species that live in the cave, not found anywhere else in the world. The cave goes through a process called condensation corrosion, and it's slowly getting bigger over the years. *Maybe this ongoing growth could happen to me too?*

This was a fun quick stop, a calm before the storm that would be the "Big 5" in Utah.

NOVEMBER 27, 2018

Zion National Park, Utah

We woke up in Springdale, Utah, with a plan to get to Angels Landing early. It was a bright, blue, windless day—perfect conditions for one of the most dangerous hikes in America.

Angels Landing is a fifteen-hundred-foot rock formation. In 1926, they cut a five-mile trail into the solid rock leading up to the top of Angels Landing, with panoramic views of Zion Canyon and the Virgin River where we'd be hiking the next day. In the twenty-two years before our visit, fourteen people had died trying to complete the hike. Short but steep, with chains bolted into the side next to a one-thousand-foot drop, this was one of the more challenging hikes we planned to attempt.

The cheap motel we stayed at had free breakfast, so we headed to the dining room off the front desk area before driving into the park. They offered a few options including one-serving boxed cereals, unripe bananas, oranges, milk cartons, and white bread—all laid out haphazardly on the fake granite countertops. We stocked up on Froot Loops, Honey Nut Cheerios, milk, napkins, and plastic spoons and ate in the car before leaving for the park.

It was a Tuesday, and the park was empty this early in the morning. It was like driving into Mars; the red rock slot canyons towered over the desert-like landscape, engulfing me like a security blanket as we drove the winding road that hugged the base of the canyons. Once at the trailhead, we found a parking spot easily and started walking.

The hike started level enough, but there was absolutely no shade to be found in the beginning. The weather was already hot, and my mouth was dry. I hoped I could make it to the top.

We passed a brown sign that read "Refrigerator Canyon," a deep slot where temperatures keep cool year-round. We took refuge before continuing, grateful for nature's little gifts.

After just under two miles of walking up a slight incline, we stopped and stared up at a series of twenty-one steep, 19-percent-grade switchbacks lovingly named Walter's Wiggles, the last hurdle before Scout Lookout—where many people not willing to chance traversing the chains would stop and turn back. To my surprise, I tackled the wiggles easily, only needing to stop once for a break. I sat down to catch my breath when I reached Scout Lookout. We shared the flat surface with a few others filling up on water and debating if they were going to keep going or make the trek back down.

"This isn't bad," I said to Shaun, pleased with my progress.

We left the safety of the wide ledge and pulled ourselves onto the narrow ridge spine, climbing an almost vertical five-hundred feet. I grabbed onto the various chains, guardrails, and carved steps as I crossed the balance-beam-like natural bridge to the sky. Realizing my upper body strength was a lot worse than my new muscle-shaped legs, I found pulling my entire body weight up on those sketchy chains was harder than the rest of the hike by far. On one particularly sloped ledge, I made the mistake of looking down to the ground, almost fifteen-hundred feet below. My legs started shaking, and I was fully aware of how easily I could make a mistake and how quickly things could go wrong.

I steadied myself and continued to reach up over my head, finding natural footholds in the rock and forcing myself to trust the well-used chains bolted into the mountain. That adrenaline was back—the kind I only felt when I was doing something extra dangerous or seeing orcas in the wild. I sighed, adjusted my gloves, and kept climbing. My arms ached, and I felt whatever strength I had melt away with every move.

Soon enough, we were pulling ourselves up to the summit, which was empty aside from one couple on the far north side. I couldn't believe our luck. Having the Angels Landing summit practically to yourself isn't something that happens often. In fact, park officials have had to limit the number of visitors with reservations and permits, because the number of people visiting is exponentially higher than ever before, creating even more dangerous and crowded conditions.

My legs were shaky and wobbly on the summit, so I lowered myself to crouch on the ground. I scooted over to the edge and looked out over the dramatic landscape. More than 250 million years ago, this area was covered by a body of water. Over the years, enormous rivers carved their way through the rock, leaving behind one of the largest deserts on Earth. The cliffs that now fill the park once started as desert sand dunes. Today, Zion has some of the most scenic canyon views in the country, delighting hikers with towering pine and juniper-covered plateaus, narrow sandstone canyons, the winding Virgin River, and countless seeps, springs, and waterfalls.

The Earth looked as if it were sliced in two, and I was sitting in the very middle. At almost six-thousand feet, I had a jaw-dropping 360-degree view. To my left, the red rock rose high, and the road we'd driven on to get into the park winded through the valley. To my right, the Virgin River surged below, protected by more red rock up above.

I just accomplished one of the most dangerous hikes in America with relative ease, and this is my reward, I told myself. I felt fit. Strong. Unbreakable. I was pushing myself to limits I never had before, seeing things I would never have seen. A wave of appreciation flooded my body, making me more thankful than ever for the opportunity to try and figure out my life in this way.

The hike down was quicker, but not any less dangerous. Soon we were back in the car, ready for the next adventure. But before we could start, we needed gear. We planned to hike the "Narrows" the next day.

The Narrows is the narrowest section of Zion Canyon, with walls a thousand feet tall and the Virgin River sometimes just twenty to thirty feet wide. The trail goes upstream, putting hikers through the river for miles.

The weather was mild for almost December, but we learned that the river was freezing. We needed to rent a dry suit complete with booties and a large, strong hiking stick to complete this dangerous hike during the winter. We made our way to the equipment rental, Zion Outfitter, and walked up the fairy-lit stairs. An employee showed us to the fitting room where we tried on different sizes of dry suits and waterproof neoprene boots.

A sign-up at the front of the store indicated all different sizes of my favorite brand of water bottles were 50 percent off. We had several water bottles, but my only Hydroflask was large and much too heavy when full. I needed something lighter to carry in my hiking pack. I browsed the selection of bright, fun colors, my eyes landing on a midsize teal blue. I grabbed the bottle off the shelf and added it to the arm with my rented dry suit.

"What's that?" Shaun asked, seconds later.

"Oh, I like the size of the yellow bottle you have," I said. "I'm going to get this, so I don't have to carry forty ounces on a hike." He walked over to the sale display, running his hands over the smooth, cool, coated bottles.

"Can I get one too?" he asked.

"What? You have like four or five of these," I protested. "You don't need one."

"But these are never on sale," he said. "Plus, my yellow one is an off brand. It's not as good."

"Even on sale, these are expensive," I reminded him. "You've been doing fine with what you currently have."

"But you're going to get one?" he challenged.

"Yes."

"Are you serious?" His voice was getting a little louder.

"Yes, Shaun, I'm going to buy this bottle for myself."

His eyes narrowed, and his expression changed from hopeful to disgusted.

"That's not fair," he argued. "I need one too."

My mind raced back to the first month of the trip, back in Montana. He wouldn't speak to me for over a day when I wouldn't buy him a collector's pin. *What's in store for me this time?* I stared at him for a minute in disbelief, trying to make up my mind if I wanted to keep saying no or if I wanted peace today. I already knew how this would play out if I kept denying him, but my stubbornness wasn't budging either.

"You don't need one, and I'm not getting it for you." I made my way across the store to pay for my stuff. "Get it yourself if you really need it." No response. I looked back over my shoulder, expecting him to follow me to the front counter, but to my surprise, he stayed by the sale display, continuing to browse through the different color options.

"What about black?" he asked.

"Yeah, that's cool," I answered, relieved he was going to let it go and buy it for himself.

"So you'll get it for me?" his face lit up like a small kid's on Christmas day.

I didn't know what to say, so I said nothing.

"What the hell? Come on!" he hissed, clearly realizing his begging wasn't working.

I walked up to the counter, paid for our rentals and my new water bottle, and walked to the exit. "Yeah. Come on," I said, gesturing to the door. He didn't budge, so I opened the door and disappeared outside, relieved to escape Shaun and the eavesdropping employees. My face was hot with embarrassment and confusion. I wanted to disappear.

Instead, I loaded the red and green dry suits into the back of my car and got in the driver's seat, blasted the heat, and waited.

I waited and waited, not sure how long I should sit alone before going back to the cheap motel without him. Finally, I walked back in, not at all surprised to see him still near the water bottle display.

"Shaun. Let's *go,*" I whispered. "What is wrong?!"

He gave me a blank, cold stare and barged past me to the front door.

"You're going to push me away," he said under his breath.

"What?" I asked, knowing full well what he said but not at all understanding his behavior.

He walked down the stairs and to the car in silence, looking at the ground while waiting at the passenger door. *Here we go again,* I thought. *Another awkward night of the silent treatment because he didn't get his way.*

I sighed and climbed into the driver's side. "What do you want to do for dinner?" I asked, changing the subject, desperately wanting to avoid an argument, hoping he would get over it so we could continue the night in peace.

No response.

"Are you hungry?" I asked.

Silence.

"OK," I answered myself. "I am. I'm going to get food from the place across our hotel."

I put my car in drive and started the five-minute trek down the main road. Shaun was staring silently out the window, and I stopped trying to ask questions or make small talk. After what felt like hours, I pulled into the tiny little café's parking lot, grateful for a chance to break the awkward moment. I got out of the car and closed the door behind me, realizing he wasn't following. It took everything in me not to keep pushing, to keep asking what was wrong or why he was acting like this. I kept silent and walked to the restaurant by myself without looking back.

I was seated at a table in the corner of the café after telling the waitress it was only me. She brought me a laminated menu and pointed up to the chalkboard where the daily specials were listed, half erased. I ordered a Cubano sandwich with fries and debated on ordering another for Shaun. We hadn't eaten since breakfast, and I knew he had to be hungry after summiting Angels Landing. I decided against it and waited for my food in peace. This kind of silence was nice.

I checked my phone a few times, wondering if I was going to get a text from Shaun, but I never did. I opened the browser and typed in "adult tantrums when they don't get what they want" and swiped through the results, fascinated but not surprised at the information that came up. Articles about emotional and financial manipulation and gaslighting dominated the top results as my Cubano came.

I chewed the crispy, gooey sandwich thoughtfully, intrigued by this new information. I thought back to the magnets and pins in Glacier National Park. Back to all the things I couldn't seem to do right. Does this explain it?

I took my time finishing the last bite and paid my bill; it was the first solo meal I'd eaten and paid for since the trip began in August. I felt extremely free and independent, but most of all I felt validated. I felt empowered, like I held some sort of top-secret information that would make my life easier moving forward. I walked back to the car confidently, ready to have a conversation about what happened at the store.

Shocking no one, Shaun didn't even look my way when I opened the door, and the icy atmosphere quickly changed my mind. I knew I made the right decision not to order him a Cubano for dinner. I drove home without saying anything. He made ramen noodles when we got back to the motel, and I showered and passed out—ready for another full day, even if it was with a child in tow.

NOVEMBER 28, 2018

Zion National Park, Utah

I woke up to another early alarm and beautiful morning. I'd slept through the night on my own lumpy double mattress, and I felt like royalty—stiff, sore legs and all. I rolled over to see if Shaun was awake, but he was still sleeping, facing away from me. I wondered how long he was going to ignore me, but I decided I was fine with the silence if that's what he wanted. He ate his microwaved ramen in his bed and spent the rest of the night passive-aggressively dropping hints that he was still upset with me, making sure I knew. I did.

I used the bathroom and started layering on my hiking gear to go under my dry suit. Conditions in the Narrows could change dramatically out of nowhere. We needed to be alert to the possibility of flash flooding, when snowmelt or rain from a sudden downpour would funnel through the canyon, sweeping unsuspecting victims to their deaths. "This can happen anytime," the salesperson at the store told me yesterday, "and the canyon can fill within seconds."

I'd never hiked up a river before, but I was excited to check something new off my list. We were planning to go as far as Big Spring, five miles from the beginning of the trailhead, with a total of ten miles roundtrip. The Virgin River's water level fluctuates from year to year and day to day.

In the fall and winter, hiking becomes more difficult, with knee-deep crossings on the slippery, uneven river bottom and frequent chest-deep pools.

We arrived at the trailhead early. Not many people were around in this type of weather. I pulled out the black-and-green dry suit, boots, gloves, and hiking stick that was supposedly going to help me trudge through the slippery rocks and uneven terrain. Sliding into the gear was no easy task, and I was sweating before the hike even began.

After what should have been a brief hike to the bank of the shallowest spot, it was time for one of us to make the first move. Neither of us could walk easily; it was more like a wobble to the river's edge. I felt like a doughboy or perhaps someone in a fat suit. I had no idea how I was supposed to hike several miles up and down a river in this.

We doubled over in laughter at our appearances and tried to get used to our new bodies. Things seemed to be back to normal again. Nobody mentioned the incident from the night before.

We walked into the river together, and I screamed as the water level rose to my knees. Using the hiking stick to steady myself, I slipped backward a few steps. These rocks were no joke; I could barely stand in a light current.

When I finally felt like I had a good, solid stance, I slowly looked up, allowing my eyes to adjust to the light while they followed the orange, towering canyon walls to where their tops touched the sky. Nothing else mattered at that point—just me and the Earth. I felt both claustrophobic and completely free, a confusing but profound feeling.

It didn't last long, because I was on my ass after a few seconds of reflection. Shaun stuck out his hand and brought me to my feet. "Ready?" he asked.

I nodded. "Let's go."

We spent the next six hours on one of the most physically demanding, risky, and adventurous hikes in the United States.

Traveling upstream against the current was even harder than I thought it would be. The boots tripled the size and girth of my feet, making each step more exaggerated than the next, but incredulously, after some practice, I was able to slowly glide from rock to rock with my walking stick as the stabilizer. I couldn't see my feet under the water, making the possibility of being pinned in between rocks and breaking an ankle very real. I had to trust my instincts more than ever with the towering canyon walls engulfing my vision and embracing both my peripheral and straight-ahead attention. The one sign of outside life appeared only when I raised my head to the sky. I could feel the piercing water through the dry suit, but I stayed perfectly dry.

Struggling up this river went against every survival instinct I thought I had. Each intense step resembled the weight of my grief, but I wanted nothing more than to keep going. I needed to see the end of the tunnel, needed to find out where this journey was taking me. I had never felt so physically strong, thinking back to when one steep hill had been enough to intimidate me back into the tent. What I now felt emotionally was a different story.

Random waterfalls lined the canyon walls, dumping fresh water into the river we were immersed in. We hadn't seen anyone else since leaving the riverbank. This place was ours.

"Cyn, watch!" Shaun's childlike excitement bounced off one wall and onto the next. He pushed off the sandstone, falling backward into the freezing water, and floated down with the current. We were in the deepest part of the river where the canyon walls were the highest and the rapids were the strongest. His red dry suit expanded with air, and he looked like an overfilled floatie as he raced by.

Soon I followed, pushing off the canyon wall and twirling with the water. My body was submerged but I was warm, and the sunrays from the top of the canyon cut through the darkness like a strong flashlight.

I lost count of how many times I slipped and fell on the way back, but miraculously, we finished the hike without injuries. Going downstream was much easier and took less time, but my ankles and calves were crying miles before the end.

Six hours later, freezing and dripping like wet dogs, we finally scrambled out of the riverbank and back onto flat land. We stripped off our soaking suits and boots, shedding some of the weight of the exhaustion that plagued our bodies on the walk to the car. I drove us back to the outfitters as the sun set behind the rocky red canyons. I pulled up and put the car in park.

"Be right back," I said as I gathered our gear to go in alone. I didn't want a repeat of yesterday.

After returning the suits, my eyes landed on the water bottle display. My heart started to beat a little faster. *We had such a good day; I should get Shaun the bottle. What harm could it do? He would be so excited if I surprised him. Maybe he won't ask for anything else if I get him what he wanted.*

I grabbed a black bottle, being careful not to make eye contact with the cashier. I was so embarrassed for no reason, like they were secretly judging my choices. I felt like both a failure and the best friend anyone ever had. Annoyed at myself but looking forward to the surprise, I left the store and made my way back to the idle car.

"Hey," I greeted Shaun shyly. "I got you this."

He looked down at the bottle before his eyes met mine. He leaned over and took my body into his, stroking my tangled hair as we embraced.

"Sorry," I apologized, with tears in my eyes. *What am I sorry for? Why am I apologizing?*

"Thanks," he said, breaking the hug and grabbing the bottle. "You're the best. I'm glad you're here."

We picked up Cubanos from the same place I ate at the night before. I felt guilty but good as I drove back to our cheap motel room. We were leaving Zion and heading on to Arches National Park, and I needed all the sleep I could get after the last few days.

"I left the bottle behind."

"What?"

"I said, I left the bottle behind."

Shaun was driving. We were an hour or so into the two-hour drive to Bryce Canyon. I stared at the profile of his face. *Was that a smirk?*

"I don't understand," I said. "On purpose? Why would you do that?"

"No, not *on purpose*," he sneered. "Why would I do that?"

I didn't know. I didn't answer.

"Maybe I'll call the motel."

"We're an hour away," I protested. "Just forget it."

We did.

DECEMBER 3, 2018

Bryce Canyon National Park, Utah

The road was washed in white. Snow drifts over ten feet high towered on either side of the narrow road. I followed the previously plowed trail, barely sneaking through. Dead branches and twigs screamed as they snapped and slashed across my car, leaving behind millions of micro-scratches in the dark gray metallic paint.

I pulled up to our shelter for the night. It had been a long, slow drive to get to the yurt. It was the only thing I could see— the only thing that wasn't covered in layers of snow and ice, nestled at the bottom of a large hill. The rounded sides of the building were a forest green, probably to help camouflage its existence in normal conditions. The roof came to a rounded point with a clear glass bubble window for stargazing on clear nights. A few feet to the left of the structure were a wooden outhouse and a stack of semi-sheltered split wood. The snow was several feet high, and we'd have to make our own trails to the bathroom.

It was only in the teens and would drop to single digits after sunset. The windshield wipers kept rhythm as they swept left and right, clearing the fat flakes before they accumulated on the window. Waiting in the idling car, I didn't want to leave its warmth or familiarity or run though the deep field to get to the rickety wooden door.

Shaun and I locked eyes and gazed back out at the yurt. The conditions were too harsh to sleep in the tent, but I didn't know how this flimsy structure could be much better. We grabbed our backpacks and sleeping bags and made a beeline across the snowfield to the front door. I grabbed the key that hung from the door and stepped into the dark concrete tent. I switched on the single lantern that hung from the ceiling, and it illuminated the large empty space.

A wooden table sat directly in the middle, amidst two mismatched chairs and a wobbly bench. Behind the table sat a wood-burning stove with a hefty stack of cut wood for burning. A single counter acted as a tiny kitchen, with a large canteen of fresh water and a few pots, pans, and washing bins. Two large bunkbeds sat next to each other on the right side of the room. The floor was concrete and had a dirty, red bathmat next to one of the bunkbeds.

It almost felt colder inside than out. We immediately started getting a fire going, hoping it would warm up the place in more ways than one. The drive had been almost completely silent, my mental energy completely drained.

The evening dragged, and the snow started to settle.

"I need to get out of here," Shaun said. "Do you want Subway for dinner? I saw one back in Panguitch."

Subway sandwiches had become our go-to easy dinner in Utah; for some reason Subway was everywhere when everything else wasn't. Even the most remote places in this state seemed to have the iconic green and yellow logo around the corner.

"Sure," I said, handing him my credit card. He'd be gone for a while, and I was surprised he'd chosen to go out again rather than make something quick with the makeshift kitchen in the yurt. Either way, I was glad for some alone time. I grabbed one of the *Travel Bryce Canyon* magazines on the table and climbed up on one of the top bunks.

The stove kept the yurt warm as long as one person stayed around to feed it every hour. The heat rose to the top of the tent dome, and my skin soon became wet with sweat. I stripped off some layers and decided to try to use the bathroom to cool off. I slipped on my black snow boots and grabbed the flashlight by the door.

It had at least stopped snowing, but the snow was almost knee deep. I'd have to plow through to make a path to the wooden toilet house. I took a deep breath and hopped into the snow, dragging my legs and feet enough to tunnel my way through. After I carved the way, the trek would be easier for the rest of our stay.

I fumbled with the door lock as the snow melted and dripped off my lower body. Once inside, I noticed a note taped to the door: "Please pour antifreeze in toilet tank to flush toilet. Toilet takes about ten minutes to fill after flushing. Please be patient. Thank you!" A jug of antifreeze sat next to an orange plastic bucket filled with sawdust and a scoop inside. I followed the instructions and waited, freezing cold and wet, to make sure it flushed and filled correctly. It didn't. It had been so cold these last few days, I wondered if the pipes were frozen. I wasn't sure what to do, so I closed up the bathroom area and trudged my way back through to the warmth of the yurt and climbed back onto the top bunk to read about the highlights of Bryce Canyon.

Shaun walked back through the door soon after. I was sad my alone time was over, but I was still happy to see him, and the sandwiches. We ate our footlongs at the wooden table in the middle and discussed our plans and hikes for the next day before falling asleep early.

I woke up shortly after to a freezing cold, dark yurt. The fire in the wooden stove had burnt out, despite stocking the stove with as much wood as possible before going to bed. I climbed down the top bunk in the pitch black, trying not to wake him. The concrete floor was ice cold on my feet. I realized we only had a few split pieces of wood left in the stack next to the stove, and I'd have to go back outside to grab some more logs from the outdoor stack.

I pulled on my boots and jacket slowly to reduce the noise I was making during the silent night and slipped out the front door. Drenching another pair of pants, I walked toward the outdoor wood stacks and piled on as many logs as I could fit in one armful. The nearly full moon lit a path back to the yurt with its filtered beams as I struggled to open the door. Once inside, I stacked the wood and started a new fire, staring into the flickering orange glow and warming my hands by the growing flames.

I had no idea what time it was, but I had to pee again. I dreaded walking back outside through the knee-deep snow to the bathroom that didn't even work. My eyes darted around the room. Maybe I didn't have to; maybe I could improvise. I spotted a large, plastic, gray washing bin stacked neatly on the free-standing kitchen counter among pots, pans, and other kitchen gadgets. I got up quietly and grabbed it, shooting a glance at Shaun to make sure he was still asleep. I brought the bin over to my bunk bed and placed it on the red mat on the concrete floor. I slid my pants down and squatted over the bin, sure this was the better option.

"Shit!" I whispered forcefully, trying to frantically rearrange the bin when I saw I had missed it entirely, peeing on the floor for the first couple of seconds before realizing my mistake.

He rustled in bed and looked straight at me. I froze, hoping he wouldn't be able to make out the shape of my body in the still darkness.

"What…are you doing?!" He erupted with laughter, fumbling for his phone to turn on the flashlight.

"No, don't!" I begged. I had nothing to hide behind, nothing to cover me up. A spotlight highlighting my half-full pee bin and wet floor wasn't exactly what I needed at the moment, but a second later, my naked bottom was illuminated, and I was on display in a not-so-flattering way.

"Cool, thanks," I hissed angrily as he belly laughed in his bunk bed. "I'm glad you think this is so amusing." I cleaned myself up and dumped the contents of the bin outside on the side of the yurt. I'd deal with the rest tomorrow. Now, I wanted to be unconscious.

I climbed back onto the top bunk and burrowed into my sleeping bag. I felt less vulnerable there. I had closed my eyes and started to drift off when I heard Shaun giggling across the room. His shaking laughter caused me to join in, our uncontrollable snorts intertwining, forming a symphony of hilarity.

DECEMBER 13, 2018

Arches National Park, Utah

We spent the last few days exploring Capitol Reef and Arches national parks before heading to Canyonlands to complete the "Big 5" of Utah. But before leaving Arches, we napped all day at our home base in Moab in preparation for the Geminid meteor shower, which peaks December 13 and 14. The Geminids travel over one thousand times faster than a cheetah and have a green hue as they streak across the sky.

My alarm went off at 1:30 in the morning and I woke up begrudgingly. Everything inside me was screaming to roll over and go back to sleep. It was freezing cold, and we'd warmed up our rubber water bottles with boiling water from the electric kettle. It stayed nice and toasty in my sleeping bag, and I was hesitant to leave it. Instead, I shook Shaun awake, and we both got ready like zombies.

I yawned as we piled into the car, and Shaun quickly copied. It was a calm, crystal-clear night, exactly what I'd hoped for. Our goal was to drive as north as possible away from Moab to the highest drivable part of Arches, Panorama Point. The long, winding road displayed red rock with white caps across a bright blue sky by day, and dark, looming arches under a sparkling dark sky by night, transforming into a mysterious, almost menacing backdrop.

We pulled up to Panorama Point after about thirty minutes of sleepy, slow driving, stopping at a twenty-four-hour gas station at the beginning of our journey for a caffeine fix before entering the park. We were the only crazy ones up here in twenty-degree weather on a Thursday night, and the quiet, still air only added to my drowsiness. It was 2:30 a.m. The crescent moon was dim and the sky was black, highlighting the glittering silver stars and Milky Way above. We turned off all our lights and electronics and sat back in the leather car seats, soaking up the residual heat from the heated bottoms. It would be 3 a.m. before our eyes adjusted correctly to the dark, allowing our strongest night vision to take over.

When the last of the heat seeped out of the car, we bundled up in fleece blankets and extra sleeping bags, stuffing hand and feet warmers into our boots and gloves. We unrolled Shaun's black yoga mat and sat on the icy asphalt before laying our bodies down together, facing the horizon.

My skull barely hit the pavement before a large, long meteor shot across the length of the open sky directly above my head. I felt Shaun gasp; he saw it too. I looked over at him, and his dark eyes lit up in a warm glow as a huge, bright fireball flew by like it was being thrown by a Greek God during a mythical baseball game. One after another—some little, some long, some quick, some slow. Every single meteor and shooting star was unique over the dark mountains and rock silhouette backdrops.

I wondered where Wayne was right at that very second. These meteors gave me so much hope that I'd be with him again someday.

"How do you think the Earth will end up dying?" I asked Shaun. "Do you think we'll go out like the dinosaurs after one big meteor, or will we kill ourselves off slowly? Why do you think we're here?"

"How high are you?" He laughed but humored me anyway. "I dunno why we're here. I've never felt like I belonged anywhere. I've never had a real purpose."

I was sad for him, for feeling lost his whole life. I'd always felt like I had a purpose, a goal…until now. I used to want to keep doing better, keep providing for myself so Wayne and I could keep our heads above water and maybe stay afloat for a while. I didn't know what my purpose was anymore, with no plans for the future. Living life one day at a time was enough for now. I inched a little closer to the warmth of his body.

"It's just so…expansive. If we died right now, nothing would even change out here! Nothing cares. One of these meteors could change course at the last minute and slam right into us. Everything we've ever worked for, gone. What's the point of anything?"

We stayed awake talking about the universe on the cold pavement on the highest road of Arches National Park for two hours, until we'd counted two hundred meteors.

JANUARY 13, 2019

Most of December and January flew by in a dream of red rock as I floated about the Southwest in a whirlwind of government shutdowns, closed national and state parks, and painful, THC-filled holidays.

Hopping between cheap rooms and family members' homes after finishing up the last few parks in Utah and Arizona, Shaun and I crashed on futons in Lovington, New Mexico; camped in the middle of nowhere; stayed in a house in Albuquerque; and spent a couple of weeks on our blow-up mattress in a garage in Austin, Texas.

I worked a day at a small, family-owned Korean donut shop and learned the differences between a good and bad blueberry cake donut (the secret is double the fresh fruit); met face first with a pack of javelinas and border control agents in Big Bend National Park; and spread Wayne's ashes on the outskirts of the closed Petrified Forest, Guadalupe Mountain, and Carlsbad Caverns national parks. We continued to go on adrenaline-filled adventures while arguing about money, plans, and anything in between.

The federal government shutdown lasted for thirty-five days and was the longest shutdown in history. It put a wrench in our plans, and I felt stuck. I wanted to get back to nature as soon as possible but didn't want to leave any parks behind. I wasn't ready to keep going east, but I also didn't want to keep crashing on people's couches. We had overstayed our welcome at more than one residence, and I was tired of feeling like a burden. I wanted to be on my own again, surviving with what I had and owing nothing.

Nonetheless, I had fallen in love with Austin, surprising even myself. I wasn't a fan of the oppressive humidity even in the middle of winter, but the green space and endless live music and barbeque restaurants outweighed the negatives of the heat and constant sweaty, frizzy hair.

"Wanna see if DJ's friend can do the tattoos before we leave for Arkansas?" I had searched for tattoo artists all over the country, but none of them wanted to take the chance on my idea. Shaun's cousin knew a lot of tattoo artists in Austin, and I knew this might be our only chance to find someone willing to work with human cremains.

"Yeah, let's do it." Shaun seemed excited. "Do you think I could get this one touched up too?"

He pointed to the faded, badly done sheet-music ink on his right arm that he'd gotten done in an old storage barn converted into an unlicensed tattoo shop, from the same people who sold us the tainted psilocybin before the trip. I'd bought it for his birthday a year before, thinking it would be a nice gesture for helping me after Wayne died.

I wanted to roll my eyes. I was already paying for the small compass tattoos we'd drawn up to represent the road trip. I wanted to include some of Wayne's ashes in the ink, to highlight his presence as my inspiration and reason for going, to honor him and our love.

Instead, I nodded and said nothing, and my mind wandered back to my honeymoon in Costa Rica, two weeks before I found Wayne dead, where we spent that last rainy day in bed during a tropical storm—watching Spanish TV and ordering room service. I thought of the show we'd watched, with the woman who had a memorial tattoo with her dad's ashes mixed into the ink.

I was no longer weirded out. After living with this hurt, I totally got it. In fact, I took it as a sign. And now, a little over a year later, I was doing it for him, whether he'd do it for me or not. I'd get a part of him ingrained in me forever.

"As long as y'all don't tell anyone you got it here, I'll do it," the artist said, swiveling back and forth on his chrome and black stool. "I ain't done it before, and there's health codes, but I'd imagine it won't hurt nothin'."

"I did some research, and everything says it won't make a difference. It's just ground up calcium," I replied, handing him the blue joint container.

"Most likely, it will melt into the ink." He tapped a bit into the black ink container, and it dissolved quickly. "You ready?"

A couple of hours later, I felt like I had super ink with magical powers injected into my skin. I had a new feeling of comfort, love, and safety I'd been missing for so long. I felt more connected to the universe…stronger.

"It's like a friendship tattoo," Shaun said, admiring his own fresh compass as we left the shop. "Always bonding us together with Wayne."

JANUARY 17, 2019

Hot Springs National Park, Arkansas

"This…is Hot Springs?" I tried to keep a positive attitude, but it wasn't my favorite place. Admittedly, I hadn't done any research on this park or area of the country, so I was envisioning natural hot springs outside in the woods. I had been so happy to be back on the road, away from civilization, back into the forests.

Instead, we found ourselves wandering through a touristy town with old, impressive architecture from the 1800s. The small downtown roads were lined with bathhouse after bathhouse, encouraging visitors to spend money at their spas. The town seemed full of interesting history, but I was eager to get moving. I already knew this was going to be a quick stop.

"Let's just get a short hike in and do Wayne's ashes and move on," I suggested. We found a trail that started right outside the downtown area and meandered into the woods behind the city. We stopped at an opening on the cliff that overlooked the town of Hot Springs and the surrounding small mountains, and we performed our short and sweet ritual, which was perfected by now. Shaun took my phone, and I took my stance, recited the date and where we were, and released a pinch from the blue plastic tube. I'd been exposed to the repetitive and familiar nature of interacting with Wayne's ashes so many times that it almost felt robotic. Instead of breaking down every time I saw the fine powder mixed with the occasional bigger bone fragment, I dissociated instead. Neither was ideal, but it was easier this way.

We started back down the trail. We walked in silence for a while, listening to the wind gusts slither through the naked trees and the dead leaves crunch under our feet.

"I saw a barbeque place a couple miles back in town called McClard's. Apparently, it's one of Bill Clinton's favorite places, and they're known for a Frito pie…wanna go?" I glanced behind me.

"Yeah." Shaun was lagging, head down, searching for rocks. He stopped to pick one up every once and a while, admiring the different types of jagged limestone and other types of mountainous rock.

He hasn't learned, I thought. *Nearly escaping a felony for collecting rocks back in Wyoming wasn't enough of a lesson, I guess.*

We got back into town after an uneventful hike and drove to the unassuming white building with red window awnings and bright green and red neon signs. I opened the door, and Shaun and I walked in together.

The bustling restaurant got a little quieter. I immediately felt uneasy and noticed some people had stopped eating and turned to look at us. I hadn't seen anything like this before. *Is there something wrong? Can they tell we're high? Am I just being paranoid?* Yes, we were careful in these states. It had to be something else.

The waitress greeted us and led us across the restaurant to an isolated table by the back window. We passed a display of colorful T-shirts featuring illustrated condiments and sauces on the front adorned with Bible verses and catchphrases about God and Jesus. It was all very fitting for a Bible Belt state.

"Did you see that?" I whispered, letting my eyes drift across the room.

"Yeah," he whispered back. "It's because I'm Asian. And you're White."

"No, that can't be," I objected. *People don't care about anything like that anymore, right?*

"You're culturally inept. Look around at the type of people here. They probably never see Asian people."

"That's insane! This is right near a national park."

"In *Arkansas*."

Maybe he was right. I'd never personally experienced racism, so I wasn't sure how to spot the subtle signs. But he immediately seemed to know why the room felt a little bit cooler than it had before we came in. I didn't want to discount his experiences, so I sat back in my chair and pretended there weren't a bunch of eyes on us. I guess I *was* inept.

We ordered a rack of ribs and the famous Frito pie to share. I was surprised the staring didn't die down as time went on, and my uneasiness began to fade into anger. These people had no idea what we'd been through and why we were there. I didn't feel welcome at all.

"Good thing we're skipping a lot of the Southeast," I said sarcastically. I couldn't wait to leave for more neutral ground, and I couldn't imagine how Shaun was feeling.

We ate the ribs and Frito pie as quickly as they came, paid the bill, and left. It was time to head for bigger and better things.

JANUARY 30, 2019

Panhandle, Florida

After spending a few days in a rundown townhouse—complete with bullet holes in the doors and walls, in a neighborhood in New Orleans—I both dreaded and looked forward to spending extended time in Florida.

I knew I needed a bathing suit for the southernmost beaches, and I hadn't been this in shape in years. I was curious what style of suit would look good on me, since my body shape was changing so drastically. I had lost around fifty pounds since August, and most of my clothes hung off my body in an unflattering way. There was a Target near where we were staying for the night, and we needed to stock up on supplies anyway.

"Do you need anything specific from Target?" I asked Shaun. "I'm going to run there quick and see if I can find a suit for all the swimming we'll be doing soon." We were going to be exploring Florida for almost a month. I was happy to be in a warm place for the worst part of winter.

"Remember when we lost my earring last week?" he asked. "I'd really like to replace it so I can start wearing them again."

"I mean, I can try looking to see if they have anything," I answered apprehensively. "Do you have cash?"

He looked at me like I had two heads. "You know I don't. Don't you miss them too? Don't you want me to look good?"

I winced. "I'm not buying you earrings. I'm sorry you lost one, but you can get them this time."

Things had been adding up over the last few months. I wasn't planning on spending so much, but it seemed like there was always something to buy or something to do that cost money, times two. And after several days of begging, Shaun had convinced me to get tickets to Universal Studios and Disney World for a week while we visited his brother in Tampa in February. I had already been to both places and didn't want to spend that much time or money on theme parks. I knew splurging on things only meant I had to go home sooner, and I wasn't ready to face that reality yet. The truth was, I was in danger of clearing out my entire savings account accumulated from all my years of working, most of Wayne's life insurance, and my entire unemployment payment, which I received for six months after losing my job. If I kept listening to his requests, I'd have nothing left.

"I thought you wanted to show me new experiences," Shaun had said after I'd said no to his pleas for the parks more than once. "You know I never got to do anything like this when I was young. And I've been saving you so much money staying with my family lately…what's mine is yours."

This had seemed eerily similar to the other times he wanted something. And exactly like the other times, I didn't have the mental energy to argue or stand up for myself, or deal with the silent treatment that came after an episode like this. So I caved and bought the tickets.

This time, I wasn't going to give, even over something as little as earrings. I couldn't.

"What if you find an earring that looks close to the one I have left and take it from the pack and put it in your purse?"

"Like…steal it?" I asked, beginning to laugh.

"Yeah, why not?" He was completely serious.

When I was a kid, I took the odd piece of bulk-bin candy from the grocery store or a sparkly butterfly clip from a campground general store. I ate a few candy bars out of my middle school band fundraising kit (who decided trusting kids with chocolate was a good idea anyway?) without replacing or paying for them. My mom put new steak knives in my purse from Texas Roadhouse across the street after their grand opening and stowed away blue wine glasses from a luau in Hawaii. And I dined and dashed with an older, bad-influence cousin in elementary school after she told me she didn't have money to pay for the fifty-dollar meal she'd ordered for us at a *TGI Fridays* inside the dingy, local mall. My parents found out and forced me to go back and apologize to the manager, while my older cousin, the perpetrator, paid no consequences. My dad paid for the past mistakes and mozzarella sticks, and it was the last time I ever came close to stealing again.

"I haven't stolen anything since I was a kid," I chuckled. "You don't need it that bad."

He looked down silently. "It's the least you can do for losing it," he said under his breath.

"What? How did I lose it?" I demanded. *Since when were his belongings my responsibility?*

"Never mind, just go. Don't get me anything."

"Shaun, I—"

"Just *go*," he said a little louder.

I got in the car confused, angry, and guilty. *Why can't I just buy him a pair of earrings?* I thought. *What's the big deal?* Feeling like the fight was my fault, I drove to Target and replayed the situation in my head over and over, trying to make sense of where I went wrong.

After trying on countless bathing suits, I chose a black, one-shoulder, see-through piece I felt good in. I passed by the jewelry section at the front of the store on my way to check out, replaying Shaun's disappointed face in my head.

He'd really be happy and surprised if I got him some earrings. I walked over to the spinning kiosks and browsed through the options. I saw one perfect pair that almost identically matched his other set, but they were over thirty dollars.

I looked around. Nobody. I could easily slip one earring through the plastic holder and tuck it into my purse.

I began to breathe heavily and my heart beat violently in my neck. My eyes darted to my side, in front of me, then finally behind me as I looked around again. I picked up the earring set and turned it around in my hands, letting each fingertip touch the fake cubic zirconia stone.

I switched it to my other hand, repeating all the previous steps while my mind raced. I peered behind me one last time. Still nobody.

I squeezed one earring from the set in between my thumb and pointer finger, twisting the stone to help dislodge it from the packaging.

I saw someone pass by to my left out of the corner of my eye. She was definitely watching me.

I stopped twisting the earring and flipped the packaging over and pretended to read the description on the back. *Titanium. Good for sensitive ears. Does Shaun have sensitive ears? Did Wayne? I do. I can only wear certain types of metals and materials or else my ears swell.*

She was right behind me, waiting for her turn to look through the selection. *Cubic zirconia. Butterfly back.* I couldn't breathe.

Sweating, I put the earrings back on the turntable and left without making eye contact. I paid for my things and left the store.

Back at camp, I filled the snack tray and replenished a few canned goods, spices, oranges, paper towels, and batteries.

I pulled out a package of Oreos with dark chocolate filling, hoping this would be enough to turn the night around for both of us.

I laughed at my ridiculous behavior. *Wayne. Can you believe it?* I knew he'd be laughing, surprised, but also probably slightly concerned. Or maybe that was just me.

FEBRUARY 10, 2019

Miami, Florida

It seemed Shaun had forgiven me for not getting him the earrings. We'd spent the last several days beach hopping at different state parks and exploring the abandoned islands and mangrove forests of Biscayne National Park. We set up camp for a week at a city campground in Miami, which wasn't my favorite stop. It was slightly sketchy and felt even more unclean than most, even if we did have the luxury of flushing toilets.

Even the drive down felt dangerous, and I was wary of the area after a man with road rage tried to run us off the road and threw a fast-food soft drink at my windshield. To be fair, Shaun had encouraged him, slowing down in the left lane when the truck tried to pass us.

"I was already going fifteen over," he said, visibly showing his own temper as the truck tried to pass.

"Who cares? Let him pass. Who knows what some of these people will do. You know, the 'Florida Man' headlines?"

He didn't take my advice, and the two cars dangerously played games before the truck raced by, trying to nudge us off the road. He brake checked us after cutting us off, flipping us off, and flinging what was left of a coke from a nearby McDonald's. It smacked onto the windshield at seventy miles per hour, and I was furious, adrenaline pumping through my stiff body.

"Stop fucking around in my car!" I screamed, a shrill tone I wasn't used to. I was scared.

He finally slowed down after hearing the panic in my voice and we arrived to the campsite in silence.

"Shit!" Shaun exclaimed as we walked back from the bathrooms to our tent we set up under the yellow streetlamp. He grasped his left foot and winced, balancing on one leg in his black flip-flops. "What the hell was that?"

I grabbed my phone and switched on the flashlight, shining it down at the ground. A black scorpion, maybe three or four inches long, scurried away from the bright beam. Our eyes widened.

"I can't believe you got stung by a scorpion!" I whisper-yelled, helping him back to the tent.

He laid down on the queen blow-up mattress we used for stays longer than three days.

"What do we do?"

We spent the rest of the night googling types of scorpions, symptoms of stings, and if we should take him to the hospital or not.

"None of the three Florida scorpion species can produce a fatal sting to humans," I read aloud. "But the sting of the black bark scorpion is extremely painful and can cause mild symptoms."

I was relieved. Shaun, not so much. His foot was swelling and turning red. "It stings. It's kinda tingly and hot."

I poured some cold water from my water bottle on a paper towel and laid down next to him on the cold but comfortable air mattress, gently covering the sting. "I wish I could take your pain away. I'm sorry this happened."

I rested my head on his sweaty thigh and looked up at his pained expression and messy black hair. It had grown considerably since we left six months ago, now covering his eyes and forehead and draping over his ears. He could even pull it back into a ponytail. I reached up and moved it out of his face. He almost looked like a completely different person than he had back in August. I wondered if I did too. He lowered his arm and lightly draped it over my back.

"I'm glad you're here," he said gently. "What can I do to make you happy again?"

I chuckled. "Nothing."

Shaun and I had been through so much together—unrivaled vulnerability, unending challenges, and downright despair—but this was new. I had started to notice and memorize his laughter—how soft and sweet it sounded, with a hint of childlike innocence. How his dark eyes squinted and almost disappeared into the rest of his face when he smiled big. I paid attention to the way his strong calves flexed while hiking a tough incline, and how the ends of his hair would get wet with sweat and drip to the ground when we were pitching the big tent. His tenderness toward animals and wildlife and his respect for nature warmed my heart, and sometimes he would collect cigarette butts and other trash from the ground and dump them in the garbage cans at the end of trailhead. He always made sure my water bottle was full and was mostly patient with me when I was running slower than the day before. He loved to meander and take his time in grocery aisles, checking out every item and creating new recipes in his head.

I felt loyal to him, like I owed him for putting up with me. He was both my biggest supporter and the biggest pain in my ass, but he brought out a side of me I'd never met before. We fought like siblings and laughed like lifelong friends. At this point, I couldn't picture my life without him, and that's not only because of the scorpion sting. The thought terrified me, because I didn't fully trust him either. There was always a sense of danger in his presence, something I couldn't put my finger on, but my first instinct was to keep my walls up high around him. Was it guilt? Guilt that I should be here with Wayne, or at least, alone? Guilt that I could feel love for someone else, even if it was just platonic?

Or was it?

We snuggled closer together, and I pushed the new feelings deep down into my gut to deal with them later.

After a sleepless night, I packed the tent the next morning. I decided to rent a room in Miami for us to call home for a few days to get some errands done, take showers, do laundry, and lay low while Shaun's foot healed.

My car was overdue for an oil change by an uncomfortable amount of time and miles. We'd been driving for six months straight and clocked more than thirty thousand miles through the Midwest, Pacific Northwest, West Coast, Southwest, and South. I'd been avoiding another car service for a few months, but this seemed like the perfect time to finally get it done. I made an appointment for the next day, and we spent the day relaxing on a real mattress with a TV, within walking distance to stores and restaurants. It was glorious! Until it wasn't.

"I'm taking the car for an oil change tomorrow, and there's a nail place right next door. I'm going to get a pedicure while I wait. You should stay here and rest. Do you need anything while I'm out?"

"You're going to get a pedicure? Why?"

"Why…does it matter? My feet have so many calluses from all the hiking. I want to get them off."

"You don't need one."

My heart skipped a beat. I started feeling defensive. I didn't want to have to hide things, but I was growing exhausted of these constant battles. *Why did I even tell him my plans for tomorrow? Do I need to start lying just to keep the peace?*

"Stop. I'm going to get one because I want one and I can make my own decisions. It's my money; why do you care if I do this for myself?"

"You always bug me about money and tell me how much you're spending. And I've told you a million times, what's mine is yours. You're starting to push me away."

"Push you away? How can you even say that? We're literally together every second of every day. I want to do one thing for myself alone, and this is how you act? And what do you mean, what's yours is mine? You told me you don't have anything."

"Nobody ever supports me in what I want to do," he said after a minute of silence.

"I'm the *only* one supporting you right now," I answered quietly.

"Yeah, only because Wayne's not here."

A pit formed in my stomach. I suddenly felt protective of Wayne, and a little unsafe.

"What are you trying to say, Shaun?"

He opened his mouth but didn't respond. He closed it again. I started to get angry, but I was also confused. *Why is he acting like this? Why is he bringing Wayne into this?*

"Don't spend money on a pedicure tomorrow. You don't need it," he repeated. His tone was different. Demanding, even. He knew he had struck a nerve.

"I'm done with this conversation," I said firmly. "You should have flown home from Los Angeles like we originally planned.

You can look for flights back to Chicago. I'll pay for you to get home. Clearly this isn't working anymore. We argue, like, once a day. We need space."

"You want me to leave?" a tinge of sadness, or panic, or maybe both, filled his voice. "For trying to save you money? Wow." His face got softer and sadder.

My heart sank. I felt instantly bad and regretted pushing back. Maybe I was wrong. He'd helped me so much.

I softened my tone. "No, I don't know. Yes. Maybe? I just feel like you're crossing some boundaries—"

He cut me off. "Haven't you realized by now? There are no boundaries."

Was he right? Have we become so codependent that I've completely lost the person I was before Wayne died? Do I even know myself? I'd stopped making decisions and lived in a constant fog. I allowed him to take control, because I only existed on autopilot. My mind raced and my gut hurt. *Could I do this without him? Would I even continue by myself?* I'd grown so accustomed to giving someone else control of my life, because I felt so out of control. After spending my entire teenage and adult life trying to influence my path with my actions, for the first time in my life, I had let go. I had no goals, no path, no responsibility. Nothing to work toward.

But I still needed boundaries.

"Shaun. We *need* boundaries. Both of us."

"Fine. I'll look at flights, and you can finish the rest of the trip alone, like you always wanted." He turned around and pulled the covers over his head.

I stared at the outline of his body under the stark white blanket. I wondered if he could feel my gaze fixed on the back of his head. The silence was awkward, and I was suddenly aware of every breath I took. I got up and went to the bathroom.

Closing the door quietly behind me, I sat on the toilet to steady my heart rate. I closed my eyes and took several deep breaths. My head was pounding, and the back of my eyes hurt—the kind of pressure that takes over from holding in tears. I wanted to keep them in, but they started to flow anyway.

This wasn't the first time Shaun had brought up Wayne in an unrelated argument, but this time, I didn't want to let it slide. For the most part, he had been a great companion, and I didn't know what this trip would look like without him. *But at what cost?* Lately, I felt like I was walking on eggshells with every other encounter, and it seemed like I couldn't do anything right. If I said the sky was blue, he'd argue it was gray. I couldn't say no to him. If I did, he'd make sure I was punished for it. The day-long silent treatment and cold shoulder episodes were starting to wear me down. Big or small, I was afraid to contradict what he wanted to do or what he said.

He always knows best, doesn't he?

I never knew which Shaun I'd be dealing with; *is today going to be the curious, excited Shaun who's always up for adventure, or are we going to waste another day arguing in a parking lot?* Maybe some time away from each other would help save any remaining friendship we'd built, but I was ready to be on my own, and I think the universe agreed.

But then again, I could never repay him for how much he'd done and how supportive he'd been since my life changed. We'd been through so much emotionally, physically, mentally. I'd never been so vulnerable with anyone, including throughout my ten years with Wayne. I was truly a wreck, barely functioning aside from putting one foot in front of the other, literally. Most of the time, I felt like my heart could give out at any minute, and just surviving was a victory at the end of every day. *Shaun's been here for all of it*, I reminded myself. Every impossible night, every panic attack and random breakdown, every flashback, every conversation about taking myself out of this world, most of which seem to conveniently take place on cliffsides or on very high bridges.

I hadn't gone on this trip thinking I was going to hike hundreds of miles, transforming my overweight body to stronger than it had ever been physically. I'd accomplished things I never thought possible by just breathing and taking life one step at a time. One more step. And another. Through the Badlands, into valleys, on glaciers, over mountains, through rivers, over waterfalls, into deserts. *Don't think about what you lost; don't think about your forgotten future. Just keep going.*

If I could survive the last year and a half, I could survive anything.

Can't I? What else is there? I can do this alone.

I thought about how free I would feel taking the next step when only my decision mattered, when only my voice was in my head. In the beginning of this journey, I was both powerless and relentless. Weak and strong. Destroyed and determined. I wasn't letting anything stop me, so why was I letting him control my next move?

I left the bathroom and slipped into the bed next to him, my mind whirling. *If he doesn't fly home now, what will the rest of the trip look like? Will this be a turning point for his behavior? Will he learn something? Or will he pretend it didn't happen and continue like normal, like how all our other disagreements end?*

Deep down, I already knew the answers. The pattern had already been sewn, and it was loud and bright.

I lay in bed soaking up the early morning light. Shaun was still asleep. I hadn't yet made up my mind from the previous night, and I cursed my new inability to make my own decisions. Not having a strong stance was going to hurt my chances of listening to my gut.

I was suddenly thankful for my dreaded oil change appointment; I needed all the space I could get, so I could be alone with my thoughts without anything else influencing my choices. I hadn't been truly alone in months.

"I love you."

The abrupt words cut through both the morning peace and my intrusive thoughts.

What?

"Yeah," he answered my unspoken thought. "I'm sorry I got upset about the national park pins and finance issues. I felt left out with you taking something back for memories and felt humiliated and self-loathing for not having the means to fund myself, so I shut down like I always do. I'm sorry I'm such a dummy and lost the water bottle in Utah. I'm sorry about it all. I wanna experience the world with you, Cyn."

It must have been hard for him to apologize, since that was usually my role in the circumstantial situationship. He sounded sincere and I desperately wanted to believe him, but my hurt was still raw from the night before. I, of course, loved Shaun too—in my own way, as much as I could love another person in such a state of mind—but I hadn't told him so. Thinking back to the night of the scorpion sting and the arrest back west, I hadn't felt that worried about someone else in a long time. It felt good to care of someone other than myself, as I'd been so focused on *me* for so long.

"I'm going to be late for the appointment. Let's take today to think things through separately. I still don't know what to do."

"Are you sure you want to go alone? You know what happens to you when you're alone out here."

Smooth. "I'm leaving. I'll see you later." I grabbed my things and left the garage apartment.

I arrived at the auto shop and dropped off my car before walking across the street to the nail salon with the neon sign. The little bell rang loudly as the door shut hard behind me. It wasn't glamourous, but the massage chair pedicure stations and smell of nail polish remover were comforting. I smiled, remembering all the times Wayne and I had gotten pedicures together.

"Pick your color," said the woman at the counter. I chose a neon pink shade after eyeing the rainbow wall of polish. She led me to the back of the salon, and I instantly felt a freedom that was foreign to me. I almost felt defiant, like I was blatantly rebelling against a strict father figure by going against his word. I hadn't allowed myself such a luxury since Wayne died, and it felt good to make my own decisions, even if it might cause friction later. I was going to enjoy it while it lasted, and I admired my tired feet as they soaked in the warm, soapy water. These feet had taken me all over the country, and they deserved some love.

Wayne had loved my feet, and I liked them too. They were dainty and feminine, my mom often joking I got her feet while my sister got my dad's. They were always something I wanted to show off, wearing flip-flops well into the Midwestern wintertime.

I deserve love too, I decided, *and this is how I'm loving myself today, in this moment. It's OK to spend money on myself, and it's OK to take care of myself.* My attention landed on an advertisement on the bulletin board that hung on the beige wall of the salon. "Skydive Key West: The thrill of a lifetime. Jump into paradise at Skydive Key West! One of the world's top ten skydiving destinations. This unforgettable experience will have you soaring above the Florida Keys." I closed my eyes and allowed my mind to wander, thinking a few days ahead as the pedicurist filed my rough heels.

I'd had skydiving on my bucket list for quite some time, although Wayne had a slight a fear of heights that got worse as he got older, so I knew I would be doing it alone someday. *Maybe this is just what I need to get the adrenaline pumping again.* I'd never been to Key West, and it was only two hours and forty-five minutes away from the alligators in the swamplands at Everglades National Park, which was next on the list.

It seemed too perfect to pass up, so through their website, I booked an excursion for Valentine's Day. I was in a "treat myself" kind of mood, and I felt great. My decision also decently distracted my mind from Shaun and all the drama back at the rental, even though he'd texted me several times since I left.

My toes were done, and it was time to pick up my car. I walked back to the auto shop after paying and stepped up to the counter to settle the oil change bill. "Ma'am, would you like to come to the back with us for a second? We'd like to show you something."

Ugh. I knew exactly what that meant; they were going to try and tell me something was terribly wrong and that I needed to fix it before I left today. *Maybe I should have let Shaun come with,* I thought. *Maybe then they wouldn't try to mess with me.*

"Your tire tread depth is as good as gone," he said. "It's not safe to keep driving on them in this condition."

Damn, they're really not lying about this one.

New tires were not in my budget, but I couldn't ignore that I'd been driving highway, dirt, gravel, and off-roads for thirty thousand miles over six months with stock tires from 2015.

"When can you do them? I'm not from around here, and I was planning on leaving town tomorrow."

"Now," he said. "We can get them done now."

Almost one thousand dollars later, I left the auto shop, in shock at the unexpected expense and time wasted sitting in the waiting room. At this point, I didn't know if I wanted to pay for Shaun's ticket back to Chicago. I was running dangerously low on funds and would need to be much more careful on the East Coast than I'd planned to, if I were to finish my goal.

Maybe we can try this out one more time, and if we keep butting heads, then I'll really know it's time to go our separate ways. He did apologize, after all. The least I can do is give it another chance.

I set the receipt down on the bed after getting back to our room. "Just about a thousand dollars! This is the worst timing for new tires."

"Are you sure you needed them?" he asked immediately. "Did you double check?"

"Yeah. They were still the stock tires, and we've driven thirty thousand miles on this trip, let alone the other twenty thousand before. I needed them." Why was I already feeling drained, like I had to defend my decision to replace the tires? Like I was in control of how worn they were?

"Great," Shaun said. "There goes my idea."

"What idea?" Curiosity was taking over.

"Well, I started to look for flights home, but it sucked so bad. And then I saw this." He held up his phone so I could see the screenshot he'd saved. "I know you talked about wanting to go to Jamaica someday. Look how cheap the cruises are for next week, and we're already in the area."

One hundred and eighty-nine dollars for a seven-day cruise, per person. I'd been paying that amount for food, gas, and campsites every couple of weeks. It wasn't bad. Actually, it was really tempting.

"You said you've been to most of the other Caribbean islands. Why not knock this one out when you're here and have the opportunity? We don't have anywhere to be."

He's right, we don't. Why not? We can make up that much by doubling down on freeze-dried food after we get back.

"Oh, this reminds me. I'm going skydiving on Valentine's Day," I said, clearly excited. "I've been wanting to do this for years. We have to go down to Key West tomorrow after we leave here."

"Wow, thanks for the invite," his tone shifted.

"Didn't you say you wouldn't want to do this? I didn't think you'd be up for it."

"Yeah. Can we do this instead?" he held up his phone again.

I thought about my tires and the skydiving I'd booked for myself, and I suddenly felt bad about the silly pedicure I just *had* to get out of principle. He was right, it was stupid and unnecessary when I could be spending that money on more adventures. It was all overwhelming, but I still had some money left.

I could always cut the trip shorter, I reasoned. I'd explored a lot of the East Coast, and most of the big parks were behind us. The more I justified Shaun's proposal, the more it started to make sense in my own head.

I realized this conversation was distracting us both from our disagreement from the previous night. At this point, I'd rather be booking cruises to Jamaica than arguing. Everything felt better when he was happy. I didn't dare bring that up again to sour the mood.

"Yeah, OK," I said, handing him my credit card. "If you don't mind figuring our logistics, fine."

He slipped it from my fingers. "You're the best, Cyn."

FEBRUARY 14, 2019

Key West, Florida

The drive from Miami to Key West took a little over four hours with traffic and an added stop at Sweet Delights Key Lime Pies in Florida City for the best key lime pie in the States. We'd stopped in a few times already, and we couldn't resist the local fruit-infused flavors the owner, Miss Debbie, created. Every time we walked into the small storefront, Miss Debbie brought out a big tray of samples of banana key lime, mamey key lime, sweet potato key lime, passion fruit key lime, white chocolate raspberry key lime, and her famous "love cake," a spongy yellow cake soaked in a caramel rum syrup.

A couple slices of pie later, it hit me that I was going to be jumping out of a plane later, and I thought I should be more nervous than I was, or at least maybe not stuffing my face with cream pies a few hours before freefalling through the sky.

Highway 1, commonly known as "Highway that Goes to Sea," spans 113 miles from Key Largo to Key West. Forty-two bridges jump from key to key over the Atlantic Ocean, Florida Bay, and the Gulf of Mexico. In 2009, Highway 1 was designated as Florida's first All-American Road by the US Federal Highway Administration.

As we drove, countless tiny islands dotted the open waters that ranged from clear, to green, to teal, to turquoise, to different shades of light and dark blues. We opened all the windows, and the warm, salty air filled my lungs and the car. I turned on one of Wayne's more upbeat playlists and hung halfway out of the passenger window, taking it all in. I'd been to Florida countless times, but I'd never experienced it quite like this. We'd already been driving around for two weeks, and we would spend even more time soaking up the warmer weather before heading back up north. Huge pelicans flew next to my car like they were challenging us to a race, but eventually, they'd give up and land on a steel perch while we left them behind. They'd dive in and out of the water, mostly coming up short, but one or two were victorious, swallowing a large fish whole. I didn't want the drive to end, but a few hours and a couple of Cubano sandwiches later, I was checking into the building near the beach.

Shaun hadn't said much about my solo adventure, and I was glad his fear of heights was stronger than his fear of missing out. I think he was excited for me, though it was hard to tell, as he'd been quieter than usual all day.

I signed all the waivers before my guide fitted me for gear in the lobby. I was going up with another solo woman, here to celebrate her twenty-fifth birthday, her mom supporting as spectator. I was glad I was finally crossing this off my bucket list, but I wished I could feel…more. I wished I could match her excitement, her passion. I was envious of her obvious glee, jealous she projected what she felt with such ease.

The birthday girl and I stepped onto the tiny plane, and our tandem partners hooked themselves to us. We took off and rose ten thousand feet rather quickly. The pilot told us about the area and pointed out a large shark through the crystal-clear water, mentioning they often see dolphins, rays, and other sea animals.

"Are you celebrating anything?" the girl asked during the fifteen-minute ride through the sky. I looked out the window at the turquoise water. I wasn't, and what's more, I was doing the opposite. I was trying to fill a void that could never be filled; I craved danger. Secretly, I fantasized about the parachute failing. I daydreamed what it would be like for this all to end.

"Nope, just a Valentine's Day gift to myself." I mustered a fake smile and quiet laugh.

"That's so great!" Her voice was shrill. "I'm so nervous! Are you nervous?"

She was going first. Her tandem partner opened the door on her side. "Oh my God, oh my God!" she screamed over the roaring air. "I don't know if I can do this!" I watched as she quietly talked herself into it, then out of it, then into it again. Suddenly, she was gone, and I could hear her screams get more faint as the seconds passed.

"Ready?" my tandem guide asked, gesturing toward the open door. We scooted over to it together, and I leaned over, looking down at the water and adjacent green land below. The rush of air through my throat took my breath away, and wow. It was a long way down. I looked back and nodded, then threw myself out of the plane, doing a front flip by tucking in my feet like how he'd instructed.

It shocked me how hard it was to breathe, and remembering to keep my head up was almost impossible, even though my tandem guide had mentioned it more than once. I spent the first ten of the forty seconds of freefall looking down at the ground until I remembered to look up and out. When I did, I felt completely weightless, and overall relieved. My weight on this Earth did not exist, and I'd given up all control and trusted my body to make the right choices. We tumbled through the air, falling freely.

I thought about Wayne, and if he was up there with me, or up in the clouds—if he was watching. I wondered if he was proud of me for being spontaneous, for saying yes. For going out of my way. For living a little, for once.

"Pull the lever!" the guide said, bringing me back into reality. A painful jolt ran through my body as the parachute opened and our falling bodies came to a halt midair. My thighs burned and my groin ached from the impact. They hadn't warned me of this. Or maybe it was my thick thighs that caused the pain.

But oh…suddenly, I had wings. Coasting through the warm, humid air, my human body transformed into a directionless bird on a windy day, going wherever the gusts wanted to take me.

"You wanna steer?" my guide shouted. "It's easy!" He explained how to move my body and arms to guide us. I took control and felt powerful. Remembering to look around, I saw the entirety of Highway 1, the dense forests of the Everglades, the famous Seven Mile Bridge, and the world's third-largest coral reef. Once again, I felt so small against the expansive Earth, so meaningless against the diversity of the world.

Everything has to work perfectly for us all to exist here at the same time. There must be a reason I'm here, right now, at this very moment, but I'll never learn what it is. Or maybe I will someday, and all this will make sense.

We were coming in for landing fast, and I could finally make out our spectators on the ground, even though they resembled tiny ants. The birthday girl was not far in front of me, preparing to land first. I came in second, extending my legs out for a standing landing, even though the ground was rocky in reality. Shaun was standing with the other spectators around a couple of golf carts, and I ran to him from across the grass field, riding on a high after my guide finished unclipping the bright yellow parachute.

"Wow," he said, a slight smile forming across his face. "Look at that smile. How could I be jealous when you're this happy?"

He reached out to me and seemed genuinely happy for me too, and I felt proud and fulfilled, like I'd pleased him in some way. I hugged him and we watched the video he'd taken of my landing, in the back of the golf cart on our way back to the car.

FEBRUARY 20, 2019

Ocho Rios, Jamaica

The cruise came quickly, and I let Shaun make all the plans. A few days before we set sail, he revealed he'd booked a slightly more expensive itinerary that docked in more than one destination in the Caribbean. My immediate reaction was to protest because this wasn't what we'd agreed on, but I quickly realized it didn't matter. What's done is done, and I didn't want to be stuck in a tiny stateroom on a ship in the middle of the ocean arguing about something I couldn't control.

Still, the thought made my skin tingle, and I felt claustrophobic. I was angry at myself for not being more involved in the plans. *But would I have protested then?* I wondered. I didn't know. If Shaun wasn't there, I wouldn't be doing this at all, and I'd be lying if I said I wasn't excited to check off more new travels on my growing list. Regardless, it didn't feel right, and I'd started to resent the control I'd allowed him to have over my finances and decisions, while appreciating him all the same.

I shoved my conflicting feelings down deep inside and told myself to enjoy the cruise in the Caribbean. I convinced myself I was silly for being this defensive about a two-hundred-dollar price difference. We docked in Ocho Rios, Jamaica, with no set plans on where to go or what to do, and I quickly got lost in the culture and color of Jamacia—without bringing up Shaun's change of plans.

After exploring the town by foot, we stumbled upon a small market on the beach. A tiny tent in the corner displayed colorful pipes and other blown glass pieces.

"Know anywhere to get something to fill these with?" Shaun asked the man in the tent.

The man's eyes went as wide as his smile, and he immediately pulled out some rough weed in a small bag.

"Which one do ya like?" he asked, picking up a wooden one with a leaf carved into the middle. "Dis is my favorite. Hand carved."

"Sure," I smiled. "I like it too."

I paid for the small wooden pipe and the weed, and he gave us a light. We eventually ran out of the tiny amount we'd bought, so we shared the vendor's joint and passed it around with his friends from the other tents. I bought a couple more joints from him, and we left the market on the beach and hired a car on his suggestion.

The driver brought us to Blue Hole, a popular destination for swimming in a fresh watering hole, with waterfalls and cliffs to jump off and a remote warehouse where he promised we could get edibles (which turned out to be a twenty-dollar piece of sweet bread). We headed on to a secluded beach an hour down the island, away from the crowds and cruise tourists. The driver dropped us off at a tiny shack on the beach that promised authentic jerk chicken.

Shaun and I shared a plate with a pineapple margarita and walked down the deserted beach. The waves were fierce, but the water was unlike any color I'd ever seen, like a mix of dusk and twilight. We laid down on the soft sand, and I dug a small hole and dumped a teaspoon of Wayne's ashes inside. I mixed him together with the fine granules and stared out at the ocean, wondering if we would have ever made it here together.

FEBRUARY 25, 2019

"Too bad this is our last stop," Shaun said as we watched Cozumel quickly approaching at the back of the ship. "I knew we should have done the two-week cruise! This wasn't long enough."

I sighed louder than I should have.

"What?" he glanced at me.

I was finally visibly annoyed after trying all week to hold in my building resentment. Every day, he commented how it *could be better* or what we *could be* doing instead, to the point that we were going to dinner and not speaking throughout. The food could have been better, the beaches could have been better, the entertainment could have been better. The rooms were too small, and we didn't spend enough time in the ports. Whatever it was, it wasn't enough, and it kept me from enjoying the tropical weather and peaceful feeling of being in the middle of the ocean with nothing else in sight but deep, blue water. I'd thought this was going to be an unplanned and relaxing part of the trip, like a reprieve before camping up the East Coast. But it had become an uncomfortable week of stress and risky adventure instead, with a few snorkeling trips and jerk chicken meals—all rolled up into one. I'd kept my mouth shut, but now, I felt like I couldn't hear any more.

"Are you ever happy with anything?" I shot at him, knowing I was spitting poison and I'd get venom back. "Can we just enjoy the moment and be thankful we did this at all?"

"Wow, wow," he laughed softly. "We wouldn't even be doing it if it weren't for me. How about a thank you for planning everything?"

I'd predicted it before it even came out of his mouth, and as much as I wanted to keep arguing with him, we were in public, and arguing in public had become a big trigger for me.

"You're right," I bit my tongue. "Thanks for planning it."

"Yeah, sure," he answered smugly, walking ahead of me and down the stairs to land.

Shortly after leaving the ship, we were dumped into a two-level outdoor shopping center. We walked around for a while, and I searched for a magnet. There were spas where fish ate the dead skin off of feet; men charging money for pictures with parrots, snakes, and iguanas; and little family-owned trinket shops intertwined with high-end diamond shops. This part of Cozumel was overrun with tourists and chain restaurants like Margaritaville. I hated it.

We left the mall and walked through town, exploring the more local and authentic areas before arriving at the ocean and renting snorkeling masks for the day.

After several hours of diving for conch shells and following colorful schools of fish through dying coral, we made the trek back to the port, stopping to buy bottled water at a little roadside stand. It was impossibly hot, and my skin was burnt from the day's activities.

A man approached us holding an open, wooden box of cigars, trying to sell us a couple for the night ahead.

"No thanks, man," Shaun said. "But do you have any weed?"

The man's face lit up. "Sí!" he exclaimed. "Sí sí sí. Come with me. I'm Asaag." He led us through the crowded streets.

I stole a glance at Shaun. "Is this a good idea?" I asked, hesitating to walk any further. "We have no idea where he's taking us or what we're doing."

"It's fine," he said. "I got this."

After a five-minute walk, Asaag led us into a small shop with a blue awning. A large metal fan blew the hot air around as I started to sweat. The store was filled with miscellaneous junk, highlighting its tobacco pipes and one-hitters under a glass counter. "Come with me," he said. "Just right back here." He gestured to a tiny back room separated from the main store by a blanket.

My red flag meter was going off, but Shaun seemed unfazed. "Isn't this how people get killed?" I whispered, trying one last time to convince him to turn around. He ignored my pleas, and we ducked around the blanket, entering a room with four additional men aside from Asaag. Two of the five of them were clearly young boys, barely high school age.

Not feeling the safest around strange men on this trip, I was apprehensive and nervous, and it showed. "I think we could all use a little ganja," Asaag said in his broken English. He pulled out a different wooden box he'd grabbed from the shelf behind him and took out a fat joint. He took a drag and passed it to Shaun, who took a couple of drags and handed it to me. I did the same.

As we smoked and passed, Asaag told us about his family and how he'd come to own this store. One of the young boys, who we now knew was Asaag's younger brother, pulled out a huge bag of white powder. He put a line on the desk and snorted it with ease. My eyes went wide, and I wanted to leave. These boys couldn't be any older than thirteen. I'd never been around cocaine before, but I knew a bag that big was probably worth thousands of dollars. We still had no idea who we were dealing with, no matter how friendly Asaag came off. Instead of calming my anxiety, the joint we were smoking heightened my already anxious brain, and I started playing all the possible scenarios in my head.

He passed the bag to me. "Sí?" he asked through my head shakes.

"No gracias," I replied. I felt like we'd been in this tiny room forever. *What's going to happen now?* I wondered. *Will they be pissed we don't want to buy cocaine from them?*

I knew Shaun was no stranger to harder drugs. I wondered if he was interested.

He took another hit from the joint. I locked eyes with him, trying to get my worry across silently. He came closer to me and inched his face near to mine. He brought his lips to my lips, parting them gently. He blew the sweet smoke into my mouth and pulled away slowly as Asaag watched. "Lots of love," he said softly, almost sadly.

We finished off the joint after a few more passes. I hadn't felt this high in a long time. *Did they lace it?* I thought my brain was going wild. *I'm so stupid. Why would they lace weed they smoked with us?* They walked us out of the room after I'd given them some cash for the weed and grabbed a bottle of Mezcal from the glass cabinets. "Let's do shots!" one of them yelled, lining up two shot glasses on the table. Again, I was apprehensive, but I gulped down my shot and decided, *Whatever happens, happens.*

We partied for a bit more in the little shop, navigating our language barrier with ease and getting to know more about local life in Cozumel. As the evening wore on, my anxiety wore off, and I was sad when it was time to leave. Asaag recommended a local taco joint and walked us over, letting the waitress know to take good care of us.

I was relieved we were safe, which left me feeling positive for the road ahead, even though I didn't know exactly what it would bring.

MARCH 3, 2019

Congaree National Park, South Carolina

With the cruise behind us, we spent even more time beach hopping and camping in Florida's state parks before the long drive up to South Carolina.

I woke up early, trying to force my eyelids to stay closed, but they popped back open like loaded springs. I was uncomfortable. My sleeping bag had twisted and bunched up during the night, my body ached from sleeping on an uneven surface, and the knots in my side screamed as I rolled over to stretch.

I climbed out of the tent slowly and silently, greeted by a bright, sunny morning. I decided I would walk to the bathrooms and clean out the car while I was in the parking lot, leaving Shaun behind to sleep. It was barely seven. I figured I'd probably be back in the tent before he even woke up.

The walk was peaceful and slow. It was a damp, warm morning, and I took my time avoiding the mud and potholes that covered the path to the main road. I finally reached the parking lot and made my way to the pit toilet near the camper registration board. I only saw two cars in the lot—mine and an empty vehicle at the opposite end. I finished up in the bathroom and headed toward my car. I opened the back hatch and fished my toothbrush and toothpaste from my bag, setting them on the front passenger's seat with a gallon of water while I organized the trunk.

A light-blue pickup truck drove by, stopping at the stop sign for an unusually long time. I watched as it kept going straight and felt thankful it hadn't turned right into the lot where I was.

I walked over to the passenger side door and wet my toothbrush, using the old gallon jug of water we'd filled from a pump in the ground. I wasn't brushing for more than a minute when the light-blue truck reappeared, this time turning into the lot, heading slowly toward me. I felt a sudden rush of anxiety flow through my body. I watched as he inched his way closer and closer, finally pulling into the parking space next to mine, despite the abandoned empty lot.

I slowly made my way to the other side of my car, using it as a shield to give myself some privacy. I was instantly uneasy. Something wasn't right. I continued brushing my teeth, pretending to mind my own business, but my heart was racing and my palms were sweaty. I hadn't even seen who was in the car yet, but my gut was screaming at me.

I heard a car door open and shut, and suddenly a man walked around the side of the hood of my car to join me on my safe side. I looked up at him with the toothbrush still in my mouth. His dingy, ratted, dark blue T-shirt and baggy, dirty jeans sagged off his body. He looked to be in his fifties, with long, greasy, limp hair that touched his shoulders but was thinning greatly in the back. His once-white tennis shoes were gray with filth. He stared at me for an uncomfortable amount of time before either of us said anything. I glanced behind him, desperate to see someone else around. Did he have a family? Were we truly alone?

"How does the campin' work?" he asked with a Southern twang, exposing his rotting teeth. I couldn't quite decide if he was sober or not.

"The sites are in the woods, about a half mile back. You park here and walk your stuff in," I said, scanning the woods and hoping anyone—I didn't care who—would come walking by.

"Can ya show me?" he asked, pointing to the woods but not breaking eye contact.

"No. I'm busy right now, but the billboard explains everything." I gestured to the instructions by the bathrooms.

"Thanks," he grunted. To my surprise, he got back into his truck and drove away.

My heart started slowing as I spit out the last of my toothpaste and began hurriedly shoving everything back in the car. The arrangement was even messier than when I started, but I didn't care. I was eager to get back to the tent.

I'd stuffed the last bag in and closed the back passenger door when the light-blue truck came into view again. This time, I walked to the open hatch and started searching for my pepper spray or utility knife. I couldn't get into my car and drive away; we were in the backwoods of South Carolina, and I had no cell service and no idea where I was. Shaun was sleeping peacefully a half-mile into the woods, and there was nobody else around to speak of.

My hands rubbed against my rusted and dull hatchet, but it was better than nothing. I slid it from its resting spot and displayed it in clear view in the back of my car as he parked in the same spot as before. As he stepped down from his truck, his jeans fell to his ankles and exposed his yellowing white underwear. He waddled to the back of his truck, pants still down, and lowered the tailgate. He faced the truck bed, pulled his penis out of his underwear, and started masturbating while looking me up and down.

There had been plenty of times I thought I was going to die over the last seven months. I'd conquered countless treacherous, dangerous hikes, a potentially capsized boat in Deception Pass, planes on the wrong flight path, getting stuck between two rocks after falling into a creek in Yosemite, smoking weed in Mexico in the back of a coke dealer's store, close encounters with wildlife, and just plain grief. I often fantasized about jumping off sea cliffs or high bridges or swerving my car into the other lane of traffic. It would be so easy.

But I didn't think it would end like this. Looking back, I would have preferred all those deaths to getting chopped up by a deranged serial killer in the deep woods or kept hostage in his basement. I scanned the area again, hoping the owners of the car across the lot would happen to walk up. This had all happened in a matter of minutes, but it felt like hours. All I could do was wait it out and stay with my hatchet, ready to strike if I needed to.

Where was Wayne during all of this? I thought about all the times I'd credited him for my survival. *Why isn't he helping me this time?* I wondered. My false sense of security vanished as I realized the severity of the situation. I could make a run for it now and get a head start while he was still preoccupied, but I thought, *He probably has a gun. It's central South Carolina in the middle of twenty-two thousand acres of forest, a floodplain, and a swamp. Not a lot of people live here, and the ones who do are questionable at best. I could charge him with my hatchet and make the first move. I can try to run him over with my car. I can scream as loud as I can and try to wake up Shaun or bring any attention to my presence.*

I thought about my family and Wayne's family. I thought about Shaun and my friends back home. They would never find out what happened to me. I'd be locked in a basement and used for years. They would chalk my disappearance up to a suicide or an accident. Maybe they would suspect Shaun. I'd be here one minute, gone the next, just like Wayne.

"At least they're together now," they'd say. It would almost be bittersweet.

A rustling sound in the woods behind me broke me out of my death daydreams, and I whipped my head around to see Shaun walking toward us. Relief flooded my body, surprising me with how happy I was at the thought of staying alive and how glad I was that Shaun hadn't left like we'd planned.

"What the fuck is this?" Shaun asked him. "What the fuck are you doing?"

He looked at me in surprise and went to the driver's side to retrieve the knife I couldn't find. I made eye contact with Shaun and tried to signal him to be careful.

The man pulled up his pants, staring at Shaun with an absent-minded expression, and got back into his truck. He slowly backed out of the spot, looking at us through his rearview mirror the whole time. He reversed until he was sandwiching us between his car and mine. He rolled down his window and made eye contact with Shaun.

"I'm jus' tryin' to 'member how to get to my favorite Chinese buffet," he said slowly, not taking his eyes off of Shaun. "I'm real hungry."

Racism hadn't even occurred to me at this point, as I was still in shock from before. Shaun and I had gotten more looks than usual in this part of the country, something I hadn't anticipated. I thought back to the Frito pie restaurant in Arkansas. All I could think about was this guy pulling out a gun and shooting one or both of us before driving off.

"Then go find it," Shaun snapped. "Get out of here!"

The man slowly rolled his window up and drove off.

I collapsed in Shaun's arms, tears flooding my face. "He might come back. This was the third time he drove by."

"Get in the car," he said. "We're packing up."

He drove my car through the parking lot, over the grass,

and onto the wide hiking trail, which clearly wasn't made for motor vehicles. "This is faster and safer. We're not leaving the car unattended."

We were supposed to stay there for another night but agreed without speaking it was best to move on. We stopped at our campsite and broke down the tent in record speed, throwing the drenched rainfly in the back without even rolling it up. Wet and muddy, we jumped into the car and sped down the trail.

I started crying uncontrollably, partly from relief and partly from fear. In between sobs, I told him everything.

"Why did you walk all the way to the parking lot?" I asked. "You were sound asleep when I left, and it's still so early."

"I woke up and immediately had a gut feeling there was something wrong," he said. "I think it was Wayne."

MARCH 23, 2019

We spent most of March driving up the east side of the US, exploring Great Smoky Mountains National Park, Mammoth Cave National Park, and Shenandoah National Park. We weaved our way up the coast through New York and Boston, to Rhode Island and into Portland, Maine, before spending a few nights in Acadia National Park and Bar Harbor.

"I love it here. What if I moved here, or Portland? This area is so beautiful, and Acadia is so remote." We had been hiking a rocky, beach-side trail as I fantasized about where I wanted to move when the road trip ended.

"No. I don't like it," Shaun said, emotionless. "It's too cold."

"But there's moose!" I joked. "I love all the forests and open land."

"Fine. Do what you want." He picked up his pace, walking faster and faster ahead of me, to the point where I couldn't see him. I didn't even try to catch up. I enjoyed my alone time and watched the temporary waterfalls that formed on the cliffsides from the crashing North Atlantic waves—disappearing and reappearing every few seconds. I thought how proud Wayne would be of me for eating an entire lobster roll doused in butter the day before.

We stayed one more night in Maine chasing lighthouses before we crossed the border into Canada to explore the poutine, French bakeries, smoked meats, and graffiti murals in Montreal and Toronto. We came back to the US through Buffalo, New York, tried the original buffalo wings and spent a day at Niagara Falls. We took our time through Cuyahoga National Park in Ohio before resting back home in Illinois for a few weeks. We'd need to leave again for Colorado and Minnesota but decided to wait for the weather to warm, so we could take advantage of the best mountain hikes and lake activities.

I had mixed emotions about going back to Illinois, and my anxiety started to act up with the anticipation of my old life. *What if we just don't go? Spend the entire spring and summer in Colorado? I can live this way for longer. I can do this forever.*

MAY 4, 2019

Great Sand Dunes National Park, Colorado

We were on the road again in what felt like no time, and I'd quickly acclimated back to living life in my SUV. At my parents' house, I had my own bedroom and my cats. I soaked up as much as I could while I was home, but I was determined to finish visiting the rest of the national parks; I craved the freedom of road life once again.

When my birthday came, I knew where I wanted to be. We left for Denver in early May and spent the day at a wildlife sanctuary, trying authentic injera (Ethiopian flatbread), grabbing free birthday joints, and getting complimentary pieces of cake from top-rated bakeries around town.

We rented wooden sleds that came with tiny pieces of melted and re-hardened wax in Great Sand Dunes National Park, waiting until sunset to trek up the huge hills just to slide back down under a dramatic purple and gray sky. As we screamed and fell violently from the sled, we were welcomed by mouthfuls and pocketfuls of sand and new bruises. I felt like a kid again, remembering back to when my dad had taken me sledding down snowy hills in the rich neighborhoods outside of town.

In snowy mittens with frozen faces, we'd taken breaks in his warm station wagon while we sipped hot chocolate with tiny marshmallows from his old, forest-green Stanley thermos.

Being back in nature instantly brightened my mood, and once again, I was present in a way I hadn't been back in Illinois. Despite all my friends and family being in the Midwest, I wasn't sure I could stay there any longer. The difference that adventure—and the mountains—made in my life was palpable, and I started seriously thinking about starting over out West.

We settled in for the night under the black sky and a dim, thumbnail moon. The hardness of the ground welcomed me back after a few weeks of sleep in my adult king-size bed in my childhood bedroom. *Am I crazy, or did my back actually feel better after all these months on the ground?*

I decided I *was* crazy, and I fell asleep tossing and turning, trying to get comfortable on my thin but convenient sleeping pad. At least this time we had the rainfly up.

MAY 16, 2019

Rocky Mountain National Park, Colorado

We filled the month of May with colorful Colorado—exploring endless snow-packed hikes, moose-filled valleys, and spring wildflowers in the Garden of the Gods; the ancient dwellings of Mesa Verde National Park; the deep, shadowy gorges of Black Canyon of the Gunnison National Park; and the alpine lakes under jagged snowcapped mountains in Rocky Mountain National Park. Each hike was more spectacular than the last, awarding us with mini avalanches and mirrored lake views for our hard work of trudging through snow with micro-spiked hiking boots and heavy, warm gear.

Not everything was rainbows and roses though. I got a flat tire driving deep into the Black Canyon of Gunnison National Park, not realizing how bad it was until we'd reached the end of the road at the mouth of a raging, rapid-filled river. Shaun changed the tired begrudgingly, and I drove back up the steep canyon road, hoping to find an open auto shop in the small town outside of the park. The small spare wasn't the same size as my new tire set from Miami, and the engine began to overheat on the way up. I had to stop the car and pull over on the side of the guardrail-less road to let it cool down every couple of miles. The process was taxing, and I wasn't sure how much damage I was doing to my car.

We finally made it up and over to an auto shop, but it took a few days until they could replace the tire. In the meantime, we found a tiny campground to stay in until it was time to drop off the car before heading on to the Rockies.

We'd only been delayed by a few days, but I was eager to get back to exploring. I only had so much money left; the balance was dwindling by the day, and so was my confidence about finishing the road trip. The lows seemed really low, and I longed for the slow, leisurely days in the West—where time seemed to last forever and there was no end in sight. Now that I could see the light at the end of the tunnel, I felt rushed into finishing, while eager to discover the next chapter in my story.

MAY 24, 2019

Voyageurs National Park, Minnesota

After spending a full week hiking Rocky Mountain National Park's many waterfalls, dramatic peaks, and forest routes, we took our time driving the eighteen hours to Voyageurs National Park in Minnesota, the last national park on our route—home of endless wetlands, lakes, rivers, rock formations, and varied wildlife, where 40 percent of the acreage is under water and the open skies create spectacular sunsets. While most of the park needed to be explored by water, we took advantage of the explosive sky at dusk, and had a few bear sightings while driving through the scenic forests.

Not long after, though, and we were homeward bound to my hometown in Illinois for good. Back to the place where I was raised, met Wayne, and spent many years with him—growing up together. Back to the place where I'd spent my first night as Wayne's widow. Back to a life I hadn't even started yet—a life as *only Cyndi*.

By then, I'd been on the road for ten long months, and we'd driven forty-five thousand miles around North America living minimally, filling and refilling gallon jugs at potable water stations and visitor centers, eating dehydrated food and countless questionable meals from gas stations, substituting baby wipes and dry shampoo for regular showers, sleeping outside with only the sounds of nature as company, ignoring current affairs, exploring new cities and food, focusing on the present, and successfully avoiding any responsibility I used to pack my life with. I hadn't thought ahead to what I would do when I inevitably ran low on money and came back to my parents' house—right back where my life started—and where I was convinced it had ended too.

Somehow in this process, I'd simultaneously run away from my reality and taken it head on. I'd made major mistakes, desperately tried to numb my pain, and questioned any decision I made every step of the way. But I'd also transformed. I'd fed my passion and practiced real self-care. I'd put my needs above everyone else's, and I'd nurtured my mental health. I'd pushed my body and my mind more than I ever had, or thought I was capable of. I'd lost seventy-five pounds of dead weight. I'd built new boundaries and let go of old ones. I'd practiced balance.

The thought of going home to a house that wasn't mine, and that didn't have Wayne, seemed hollow. No reason, no job, no goals to work toward—it all seemed pointless.

Knowing you're taking a step backward instead of forward is never easy. The ever-present anxiety in the back of my mind reminded me of the overwhelming feeling of a future still unknown. *Will going back undo everything I've done out here?* Relearning to live a life I had once abandoned not only seemed silly, but it also felt impossibly hard. I'd adjusted to my lifestyle on the road, living each day differently with nothing but a few grief books, warm clothes, and painful memories.

What had I learned? Who had I become? *What now?*

iii. the return

> *"Look deep into nature, and then you will understand everything better."*
> —Albert Einstein, 1951

anger
hindsight's enemy
the present's guilty pleasure
it comes disguised
as heavy grief.
as it grows
everything else gets smaller
until it is all you know
ready to heal
the anger

DECEMBER 19, 2022

Reykjavík, Iceland

"Ugh," I struggled audibly. "Shit." I was stuck, in more ways than one.

It took me a couple of hours to gain the courage, but I finally got the confidence to squeeze through the tiny window between the cab and the back of the tall white campervan. The storm was roaring, and getting to the heater and water without leaving the shelter of the rental van was my goal. I let out a frustrated sigh and rolled my eyes before bursting with laughter.

I wonder what I look like right now, I thought, trying to squeeze back the way I'd come. My breasts ached with pain as I flattened my chest as much as possible in hopes of release.

"Are you kidding?" I yelled out to nobody but myself, both amused and annoyed at the situation I'd gotten myself into. On one hand, I was glad I was alone. On the other, it would be nice to have help. Imagining how this would play out if someone came across me, I tried one more time to eject myself from the tiny square cutout in the back of the cab. Thankfully, this time it worked.

The van shook and howled with what felt like the force of a million windstorms as I settled back into the driver's seat. I felt the vehicle groan and slide slightly to the right, causing panic in my throat. Just over the tiny guardrail, the Northern Atlantic Ocean was as black as the night sky, but much angrier. Fierce waves crashed in countless directions, turning the gigantic sea into a roaring boil on the surface.

Nothing separated us but a cheap piece of metal that barely rose above the crumbling asphalt—nothing that would keep me and my van from getting carried away at sea. The powerful wind had carried the snow drifts from the nearby mountains, dissipating them into powder that swirled across the tiny highway and melted into the sea. Like pure white birds diving for their prey, the drifts pierced through the uneven waters and vanished from my sight.

I glanced down past my white knuckles. About one-third of a tank of gas left. I'd been sitting there for just over five hours a few days into my trip, trapped with about fifteen other cars going the same direction. Before the storm hit, a few days after beginning my trip, I'd been trying to rush back to Reykjavík. I'd failed ten miles outside of town.

A member of Iceland's volunteer-based search-and-rescue team appeared at the window, head down and fighting hard against the wind. I attempted to roll down the window to communicate, but it was stuck shut with ice and snow. The man cleared a little peephole on the outside and held up a bottle of Icelandic glacial water, tapping it gently on the window.

That's funny, I thought. *I'm surrounded by the purest water on Earth, and they're out here handing it out in bottles.* Just yesterday, I'd filled my water bottle in a roadside stream and sucked it down eagerly, tears in my eyes as I drank directly from the Earth.

I unlatched the door and leaned against it with all my weight. It didn't budge. The wind was incredibly strong, and this wasn't the first time over the last few days where I'd struggled to keep control of the heavy doors.

In the winter, Icelandic storms frequently produce winds over fifty miles per hour, making it difficult or impossible to drive, walk, or do anything but wait them out. Car doors get blown off, vehicles fly off the road, and it's not unusual for the powerful winds to smash windows.

I locked eyes with the man through the tiny window clearing as he placed his hands on the door handle. After a short pause, I pushed and he pulled, finally creating a sizable crack to the outside world. The freezing wind pierced my skin as he handed me the bottle and gave me a slight smile. I asked how long he thought it would be, not expecting him to understand my English, but he did.

"They're almost done clearin' the road over the bridge," he said loudly in his thick Icelandic accent, barely able to outspeak the groaning wind. He almost sounded like he was from Minnesoooohtah. He was the first person I'd spoken to since the airport and picking up my van a few days prior.

"Once th' overturned cars are out th' way and the winds die down, we'll guide ya one by one over the bridge into the city. Expect a few more hours at best, and long into the night at worst," he continued.

He was gone as quickly as he'd arrived, moving on to the tiny manual sedan behind me. Despite being stranded on a remote road in a foreign country alone with no ability to see even a foot in front of me, I felt surprisingly good. Safe, even. Certainly safer than during many other moments I'd left behind in the States. I had a piece of Icelandic dark chocolate stashed away, enough water to last me a couple of days, a diesel heater, and a bed—if I could get myself back there without going outside or getting permanently stuck. I could make anything work.

The van's front heater was barely producing anything but

a dull blast of lukewarm air that chilled my skin and slightly damp hair even further. After five hours of idling my engine, the heater was no match for the piercing cold and wind outside, a drastic difference from a few hours before when I'd relaxed in the soothing, heated water at a natural volcanic hot spring in the center of the country.

I knew I was foolish for attempting to drive Iceland's 827-mile Ring Road in seven days during the dead of winter, but I was prepared to stop wherever it felt right to hunt for hot springs, chase the northern lights, and find frozen waterfalls. I planned to make it to Chicago in time to visit my family on Christmas Eve, and the short days and long nights were going fast.

The weather forecast the weeks before had looked promising, but when I was met with several feet of snow and more coming after landing at the tiny airport in Keflavík, I knew things probably weren't as they seemed.

"You alone?" asked the woman behind the counter at the van outlet on my first day in the country, meeting my tired eyes with her wary gaze. "We don't get many of you, especially this time of year."

"Yeah, it was kinda last minu—"

"Here," she interrupted, swinging her computer monitor around. "Our first blizzard of the year. Usually doesn't happen this early or hard." She pointed to the weather-warning website. "This is the only source to pay attention to. Road conditions and closures are constantly updated."

The entire country on the map was littered with little orange, yellow, and red exclamation points. Obstructed roads, blocked roads, fully closed roads.

"Check every hour," she warned. "Things change quick. Contact us through the van Wi-Fi if something happens and you need help. At least you have snow tires."

She pushed the paperwork and van keys toward me. "You'll be fine! Just don't hit a sheep. You'll pay the farmer a pretty penny and be stuck with a lot of meat you don't want…Þetta reddast!" she shouted after me with a grin and shoulder shrug as I left to find my van and camping gear.

It will save itself in Icelandic. Everything will work out. It is what it is. Life goes on.

I walked out back through the deserted front lobby and into a large warehouse, keys in hand, and grabbed a large wooden bin labeled *Cyndi,* which had everything I would need for a week in the bitter Icelandic wilderness. The rental included one duvet blanket, one fitted sheet, two pillows, a bucket of cooking tools, a five-gallon water container, and two small canisters of cooking gas. It was far fancier than what I was used to, I had reassured myself.

After practicing the traction and controls, I turned out of the van lot. It was still dark at 7 a.m., and the sun wouldn't make its appearance for another several hours during this time of year. The snow was thick and heavy, quickly covering my windshield and side mirrors even with the wipers on the highest setting. I drove for half an hour, kilometers under the speed limit. Visibility was almost nonexistent as the wind ravaged swirling snow across the one-lane road and turned the air white. I felt my van drift to the left, then to the right. I opened the driver's window and stuck my head out to see if I could see better. I couldn't.

I stopped at the nearest gas station. I'd been awake and traveling for more than twenty-four hours, and exhaustion was quickly taking over my body and mind. My heart was pushing me to keep going; the anxiety from the possibility these roads could close at any minute weighed heavily on my mind. I wanted to get out of civilization *today*. On the other hand, I didn't trust myself to continue in these conditions.

I stepped inside the gas station store and loaded up on Icelandic snacks, drinks, and windshield deicer. I left with a bag of lamb jerky, a fresh deli sandwich made with roast beef and cheese, some chocolate, and Stjörnu Osta Popp—cheese popcorn. I climbed into the back of my van, turned the tiny table into a bed, and clicked the diesel heater on high. *I'll sleep for a few hours until the sun comes up, and then I'll get going,* I decided, closing the dark-blue, stained curtains.

I woke up a few hours later. The snow had accumulated about a foot around on top of my van. I pulled my boots back on and fished out a snow scraper and the deicer.

It took me a half hour to scrape the car, but I was ready to hit the road. It wasn't quite light out yet, but I could see the sun peeking up from the horizon, and it wouldn't be long now.

I slowly left behind the outskirts of Keflavík and headed northwest to the Snæfellsnes Peninsula, hoping the snow would die down soon. I could still barely see the road in front of me, let alone the dramatic scenery I hoped to experience, but I had no choice but to keep going if I wanted to make it out of the city.

The empty, tiny two-lane highway seemed endless, and the midnight sun hung right near the horizon for most of the day, casting an infinite golden-hour filter across the landscape. The snow was patchy, with the wind blowing sheets of it across the treeless terrain, exposing dots of green moss and grass mixed with black volcanic rock. The clouds raced as fast as the wind, revealing looming peaks and jagged tips and towers that jutted out into the endless ocean.

I switched on the van radio, getting nothing but static at first, but then landed on a Christmas special in English, peppered with traditional Icelandic holiday music and stories. After a few hours of driving, I stopped early for the night and hoped for a better day ahead.

Iceland only gets about four hours of sunlight in mid-to-late December, something I knew before coming, but it gave me a leg up when searching for the northern lights. I pulled into a marked campground, which was nothing but a deserted snow field with nothing around but a small, heated wooden shack with a basic kitchen and bathroom.

Alone, the silence and deafening wind were eerie. It was still early, but the weather and darkness made me lack the energy to find a nearby place with any type of food.

I should definitely be sleeping, I thought. I was sick of white-knuckle driving and longed for the cozy, stress-free duvet blanket and down pillow in the back. I fired up the diesel heater and switched on the tiny battery-powered string of fairy lights I'd brought in my single backpack. I started peeling off layers one by one—first my insulated waterproof snow boots, then my long underwear, followed by my fleece leggings. My thermal long-sleeved shirt was next, and finally my three-layered ski jacket, shell, and face mask.

I ripped off my gloves, scarf, and wool hat as the van started to heat up, and I was suddenly sweaty. After purging my wool hiking socks, I laid back—out of breath. Just getting dressed and undressed took an enormous amount of energy I wasn't sure I had. I laid there and stared at the ceiling. The van was shaking and groaning with the wind, and the force of the gusts sounded like a freight train charging head-on. My stomach grumbled along in unison.

I must have drifted off to sleep, because I woke at 1 a.m. to roaring wind and a dull glow outside. I parted the back window curtains and used my elbow to wipe the condensation from the windows.

At first, I didn't see anything. But as my eyes adjusted more, I realized the sky was dancing.

My clothes were still in a crumpled pile next to me from before. I started pulling them on, one by one, until I decided it was taking much too long. I didn't want to waste one more second. I threw on my leggings and insulated ski jacket without anything underneath and grabbed my scarf, pulling on my boots without tying the laces.

I tried to open the sliding side door, but the wind was wrestling it back the other way. I fumbled with it for a few seconds before slamming it open with all my might, breaking the door handle off and leaving behind my warm, safe shelter. I stepped out into the blizzard, and for the first time in my life, I was glad I'd splurged on the unlimited auto insurance. The strength of the wind caught me by surprise, and I remembered stories of van windows shattering and car doors flying off. Instead, my scarf went flying, landing in a large snow drift next to my parking spot. I left it there and raised my warm, pink face to the black sky and zipped up my coat, covering my bare chest from the elements.

Bands of swirling lights—white and a very muted green— moved effortlessly, directly above my head. Horizontal pillars stretched as far as I could see. The scene resembled something underwater, like bioluminescent algae swirling through the sea on warm nights. The universe meets the ocean.

It felt good to be alone. Uncontrollable joy burst from me, and I was unable to contain my tears. They quickly froze on my now-stinging cheeks, but I didn't care. I followed the lights, running through the dark, abandoned snow field, audibly shrieking and screaming as the lights grew more powerful by the second. I forgot my gloves in the car and my fingers were frozen and not working, but I pulled out my phone anyway. I set it to night mode and held it as still as I could, waiting a few seconds while the shutter let as much light in as possible.

I glanced down at the screen. Bright green, purples, and pinks filled the photo, showing me what my own eyes couldn't quite see. I ran up a small snow-covered hill, huffing and puffing as the cold air filled my lungs. My boogers were frozen and I was in pain, but I couldn't take my eyes off the sky.

I stayed outside for an undetermined amount of time, but I still made it back to the van before I got any frostbite. After performing my disrobing routine once more, I slowly chewed the last few pieces of lamb jerky, officially going through the last of my snacks. *I need to eat some real food tomorrow*, I promised myself. I sat near the heater, allowing it to fully thaw my frozen body.

Then I fluffed up the duvet and down pillow, settling into the cozy bed. I had a long week ahead of me, and I needed as much sleep as possible. The unknown, while once incredibly frightening, now felt like home.

The morning after seeing the northern lights for the first time in my life, I woke with renewed energy and a sense of adventure. Over the next few days, I planned to repel down inside an inactive volcano, hike through a glacial cave, and snorkel the Silfra Fissure in Thingvellir National Park, a freshwater fissure between North American and European tectonic plates.

I also woken up freezing. It was still dark at 11 a.m., and the diesel heater had died overnight. I could see my breath inside my once-cozy temporary home. It reminded me of all those months I'd spent living in a tent at the mercy of the elements. I adorned myself with my winter uniform and ran across the snowfield to the heated facility, grateful for a bathroom and tiny kitchen with a chair and table.

After brushing my hair and teeth and layering up for the day, I left the campsite in the abandoned snowfield and started my way across the island. I spent most of the day driving down harrowing, icy mountain roads; over covered wood bridges;

through valleys and flood basalts; and by hidden waterfalls. I stopped at black-painted churches and diamond beaches, glacial lagoons, and national parks.

Real food, I'd learned, was pretty hard to come by on this route. By this time, my hunger was too great to ignore. I hadn't eaten anything substantial or warm since leaving the States. Not wanting to waste any time, I stopped at a random gas station in the middle of nowhere, hoping to grab another sandwich and be on my way. Instead, I walked into a cafeteria-style room attached to the gas station, which offered seasoned rack of lamb, brown gravy, au gratin potatoes, and bean salad. It was the best and only hot meal I'd have over my week in Iceland, and it was cheaper than a cheeseburger in the States.

Thankful for the warm food and full belly, I arrived in the center of the country and stumbled upon a natural hot spring. Walking up to the entrance, I realized I had the entire place to myself. I was instantly relieved, mostly because I desperately needed a shower (and you must shower naked prior to entering the springs), but also because I couldn't leave Iceland without plunging into the healing water. The forecast was getting worse as the day went on, roads were closing by the second, and it would be dark soon.

Maybe I can spend a few hours here and stay the night while I wait out the storm, I thought. That was the beauty of being alone with no set itinerary, nothing could really go wrong, because there were no pre-set expectations and I didn't have to worry about upsetting anyone. I liked living this way. Somehow, it was less stressful than planning in advance. *I'll end up wherever I end up, and that's part of the adventure.*

The valley surrounding the sulfuric springs and white mountain peaks was heavily scented with rotten eggs. The wind felt like knives slashing through my wet body as I walked up to the series of naturally heated and formed pools after my first naked public shower.

I put down my tiny microfiber travel towel at the base of the warmest pool and slid my chilled, half-naked body into 104 degrees of pure joy. The wind raced into one ear and out through the other, freezing my brain and my wet hair on the way. The contrast of sensations was overwhelming. I let out a long, exaggerated sigh and relaxed my body, dipping the frozen ends of my hair into the hot water and watching the ice dissolve. Lowering my head even more, the warm liquid engulfed my scalp, and I submerged the rest of my frigid body—before floating on the surface. The freezing wind kissed the exposed skin on my stomach, thighs, and nose. Everything was silent.

This is so much better than Hot Springs National Park in Arkansas, my mind reminisced, picturing rows of bathhouses and gift shops. A cool concept for a town, but not at all what I'd expected from a national park.

Steam rose from the scalding water and collided with the glacial air, freezing the nearby winter foliage and leaving a layer of ice on the surrounding landscape. My teal travel towel quickly became saturated with steam and froze solid in the shape I dropped it in—stiff as a board, useless.

It had started to snow, and the silence of my surroundings engulfed me almost as warmly as the steaming springs. I had a 360-degree view of rolling valleys, white mountains, and steaming streams and pools—all to myself. The storms must have scared everyone else away.

I am alive, I thought. *I'm not scared.*

Ten miles outside of Reykjavík, I *was* scared. I had made a last-minute decision after the hot springs to drive three hours back toward civilization. As much as I enjoyed my solitude, I didn't want to get hurt or be the dumb tourist who needed to be rescued.

I ended up being the dumb tourist who needed to be rescued. After a total of five and a half hours stranded with about fifteen other cars, the search-and-rescue volunteers guided my campervan over the threatening bridge. I felt the van slide to the right more than once, centimeters away from coming into contact with the flimsy guardrail that separated land from raging sea.

I was trying to follow the rugged snow-equipped truck leading me, but I couldn't see anything. I simply relied on knowing the bridge was a patch of straight roadway, remaining careful not to turn my steering wheel any which way. If I could get past this bridge, I could make it back in one piece. If I could get back to the city, I could park my van and get warm.

Eventually, I made my way back into the city at a steady pace of ten to twenty miles per hour. I found an urban campground—after a detour and a wrong turn that left me stuck in a snowbank, both of which added more time to my already exhausting trek. But I was finally parked for the night, and I couldn't wait to be unconscious for a while. I used the last of my clean water to splash my face and brush my teeth—the realization of what had just happened flooding my mind.

I could have died out there. I thought back to the dozens of cars I'd passed stuck in snowbanks, flipped in ditches, and piled up in collisions. *I've been reckless and careless and everything in between, but I'm still alive.* Overwhelmed with gratitude and consumed with both guilt and joy that I was still around to have these experiences, my mind drifted to my past life and all the circumstances that had landed me alone in Iceland, living a dream I once shared with more than one person.

Two months into living back in dull Illinois with my parents after the road trip ended, I got a job as a marketing copywriter for a company that manufactures automated external defibrillators (AEDs) in Washington state. I found a small, two-bedroom apartment with a loft that overlooked a tiny patio and a lush, green garden. With my parents' and Shaun's help, I moved myself and my cats more than two thousand miles to my favorite part of the country a few hours from Olympic National Park. My new home on the hill had a cherry-red door and shared a street with a state park and Lake Washington, the second largest lake in the state.

After the two-day drive from Illinois to Washington, I'd stepped inside the apartment under a beam of moonlight that shined between the towering trees in the backyard and into the small living room. I sat on the stairs alone and wept. For Wayne, for our families, and for myself. For everything I had lost, and for everything I would gain. My sobs echoed through the tall ceilings and abandoned rooms, and brought me right back to the staircase I'd sat on two years before, after finding Wayne's body. I'd learned so many lessons since then. How to trust my gut, when to say no, and when to say yes. How to love myself despite hating myself, and how to create healthy boundaries and coping mechanisms that balance my unhealthy ones.

A familiar disbelief had settled in, but the incredulity was intertwined with hope. After losing everything I had ever known, I finally felt at home.

At my new job, I produced survivor stories about individuals and families who suffered a sudden cardiac arrest but were saved by the AEDs, combined with CPR. Interviewing the families who still had their husbands, fathers, siblings, and children, and telling their stories of death and revival, was an odd sort of exposure therapy, and it was both cathartic and heartbreaking. Sometimes, it reminded me of my own failures. Other times, it reminded me there wasn't anything I could have done for a different outcome. I often asked the survivors how their lives and relationships had changed after receiving a second chance, searching for solace in their answers to make sense of my own story.

Shaun followed three months after I arrived in the Pacific Northwest, transferring to a Washington-based branch of his employer, and we tried to live together. But making things work in the real world outside of the fantasy and distraction we'd created for ourselves was impossible. Our relationship transitioned into a toxic, codependent whirlwind of love, jealousy, and hate, and I started resenting that he only paid me a third of the expensive Seattle-suburb rent each month and offered no help for utilities. I would often dread his return home from work, anticipating the routine he'd created of walking through the door and criticizing the way I'd cleaned, or hadn't cleaned, or what I made for dinner. I was always chopping the onions wrong or not vacuuming often enough, and the way I'd worn sweatpants during my work-from-home days bothered him so much he called me lazy, unproductive, and unattractive. Soon, I'd find myself jumping up minutes before he came home to make myself look busy just to keep the peace.

During an argument in the early days of the COVID-19 lockdown, Shaun physically restrained me from leaving my bedroom, preventing me from going to a hotel overnight after I realized I wanted time away from him to cool down. He accused me of having borderline personality disorder and told me he didn't want me to leave the house, that he needed to keep me safe from the pandemic. I tried to wiggle out of the vice grip he embraced me with—feeling threatened, scared, and unsafe around this new behavior.

He had finally crossed a boundary I wouldn't budge on. Having finally seen the forest for the trees, I played my cards carefully in the months that followed, listening to my gut that had been screaming at me for far too long, but I was in denial. I encouraged him to move out and grappled with wanting to save any shred of our trauma-bonded friendship, while he packed up every one of his belongings—down to the lightbulbs he changed out in the apartment's old, bronze fixtures, the hooks in my wall that held my hairstyling tools next to my vanity, and the fairy lights we'd hung together in the garden. I knew deep down it was too dangerous for me to continue. We stopped speaking shortly after we stopped living together, and I felt both free and fearful. I was relieved to be released from the shackles that held me back but felt abandoned and betrayed by my best friend, not to mention foolish for letting my vulnerability override my stronger instincts.

I lost myself when Wayne died, and in the process of regaining myself and my strength, I also lost Shaun, who I thought was my biggest supporter. For years after cutting off contact with him, I felt like I was healing from two deaths at once. Another important part of my life, gone. Another new life to adjust to. Another painful lesson learned.

Just five years ago, I'd sat by myself at my airport gate in Chicago, uncontrollably crying as quietly as I could so I wouldn't draw attention to myself. I was on my way to Phoenix, Arizona, for a widow grief retreat. At age twenty-eight, I was the youngest there by about twenty years, if not more. It was my first time traveling alone, only two months after we'd lost Wayne. Traveling alone was so overwhelmingly painful that even watching families look after each other's luggage while they went to the bathroom before boarding felt like salt in an already infected and festering wound.

Now, I hadn't had a full night of sleep in days. I was snowed in within a foreign country with perpetual nighttime darkness and unbelievable winter weather in a campervan I barely knew how to drive. I had no idea how long the roads around me would be closed or if I'd make it to Chicago to see my family for the holidays. I'd most likely miss out on all the adventures I'd planned. But instead of crying for what I couldn't control, I was crying for how far I'd come: from absolute rock bottom to manifesting my long-term dreams into reality, because there was simply no other way to live.

The years felt so short and so long at the same time, probably because so much and so little had changed. Eventually, Wayne would be gone for longer than we were together, and then longer than he was even alive.

Over these last five years, the earth had kept spinning, the sun kept rising, the birds kept chirping, and I kept growing. I made huge mistakes and learned life-changing lessons. Grief forced me to live every second in the present, because I couldn't focus on anything except what I was feeling in the moment. The fog was too thick; the pain was too real. Thoughts of the past were jaded, and visions of a future where I could ever be happy again were completely overwhelming, impossible, and out of reach. I was a prisoner of my own life, fighting between excruciating memories and a dark road ahead.

It shouldn't make sense, but somehow it had been easier to focus on the present, even though in many ways, it was a living hell. I'd made countless mistakes, turned into someone I (and my family) didn't recognize, and treated my life like it no longer mattered, making decisions I knew would make the hole even harder to dig out of.

But at the time, I didn't care.

That night, as I fell asleep in a city parking lot amidst a land of waterfalls and northern lights illuminating my mind, I did care.

epilogue

It took me over three years to transfer Wayne's remaining ashes from the trip into a permanent urn. I always had some kind of excuse. Couldn't find the right container, didn't want to deal with it emotionally, wanted it to be personal and not *look* like an urn. In reality, it was all part of lingering denial; a forever home is just that. Forever. And I didn't want it to be. So, I waited. And waited. And waited. Now it's done, and the denial is still there, but the guilt in keeping him in cardboard is gone.

The guilt. I grappled with it with such intensity for so long, it overwhelmed my existence. As humans, we have a primal instinct to feel in control. Guilt is a way of taking responsibility and control of a situation the brain cannot process. I easily gave others with trauma far more grace than I did myself; but I could not forgive my own guilt. Somewhere deep down, I wanted to be at fault, because that way, I had someone to blame for how our lives had turned out.

Now, Wayne exists in a delicate, circle-shaped blown glass vase, complete with a cork stopper for the top. The vase is vibrantly hand-painted—displaying blue, orange, and yellow roots that twist up into a giant tree, looming in front of a bright, full moon. His remaining ashes fill half the vase, completely visible through the scene. It's unique to this world, as he was.

Being this deep in grief for so long completely changed everything I've ever known or believed. Losing him is the worst thing that will ever happen to me, yet it transformed me into who I am today.

It's important to remember both things can be true at the same time. Losing him is the worst thing that will ever happen to me, *and* I can still live a meaningful, beautiful life. Loss has opened my mind, heart, and soul to a life full of adventure, acceptance, and adaptability. His death still drives every decision I make for my life, but now, I want to live.

When you lose your husband, best friend, job, and home all in the span of just months, nothing feels real. Nothing makes sense. I spent hours—weeks—months—years searching for answers nobody could ever offer. I didn't want to be here. No husband, no job, no home, no family of my own, no purpose. Life was so void of joy and happiness, and I couldn't picture a way out. As time passed, I didn't necessarily find anything, but I fell in love with the healing powers of nature.

And I fell in love with my own strength.

I am so grateful I kept going. Something that seemed physically and mentally impossible became more realistic as I fought to shed the negativity and toxicity in my life that was holding me back from taking care of myself and moving forward.

Forward is crucial here. As widows, we move forward, not on.

This life isn't what I had in mind, not even a little. Those plans were crushed when my world collapsed around me. I've lived one hundred different lives and met one hundred different versions of myself since then, but the only thing that stays constant is missing Wayne—and I suppose the irrevocable feeling of homesickness for a person who will never come home.

Through adversity and suffering, when life is unbearable and uncertain, our superficial desires disappear. What remains is what really matters to us: survival. Life becomes remarkably simple and its purpose is crystal clear.

The biggest lesson? The only way out is through. Through acceptance, through grace, through love, and through grief, one hour at a time. Until those hours turn into days, which turn into weeks, which turn into months, which turn into years…until your grief isn't any less, but *you* are *more.*

I am me because he lived. I am me because he died.

HELPFUL TIPS AND RESOURCES FOR NEW WIDOWS

A mix of coping mechanisms work best. Everyone is different, and not one solution fits all lifestyles. The following is a list of what I feel was most effective during my deepest depths of grief.

TIPS

1. Move your body, ideally in a natural setting.

2. Lean on your support system. Learning how to ask for help is a skill not everyone can master. Put your pride aside, and when people ask what they can do to help, remember these offers and take them up on it when you feel overwhelmed.

3. Give yourself a gentle reminder that not everything *has* to get done. There will be a lot of important things to do in the beginning, and it can feel impossible to get through your to-do list when you're in so much pain. Let all the extra "noise" go, and focus on the basics of survival: try to get enough rest, enough water, enough food, and everything else will come in time. If you have children, taking up your friends' and family's offers of help should give you a chance to take better care of yourself in the moment.

4. Begin therapy as soon as possible. Try your local police station or hospice if you're struggling with resources. Often, they can provide free sessions with counselors. Experiment with all types of therapies: eye movement desensitization and reprocessing (EMDR), art therapy,

writing therapy, cognitive behavioral therapy (CBT), and more.

5. When you feel you have enough concentration, or if there are certain times of the day that don't seem so heavy, try to read widow books or blogs, listen to podcasts or audiobooks, and join widow communities on social media. Dozens of free communities exist for people going through similar struggles, no matter what age or situation.

6. Seek out massage therapy, acupuncture, meditation groups, and grief shares. Find support groups specific to spousal loss.

7. Connect with other widows in person through meetups, classes, outings, and more. Establish a group of widowed friends who are around the same age— in similar situations with similar timelines—and who can understand your pain, and you theirs.

8. Build your boundaries, and stick to them. Being newly widowed is deeply disorienting, and the lack of self-esteem and confidence may leave you vulnerable and confused.

9. Don't beat yourself up if all you did was lie in bed today. You're doing an amazing job by simply existing.

10. Find something that makes you feel alive, and do it. Then keep doing it. Rinse and repeat.

RESOURCES

1. *Soaring Spirits:* an inclusive, non-denominational organization focused on hope and healing through the grieving process that offers members the tools and resources they need to rebuild their lives after the death of a spouse or life partner.

2. *Camp Widow:* an innovative program that provides practical tools and research-informed resources for widowed people rebuilding their lives after the death of a spouse or partner.

3. *Hope for Widows:* a philanthropic organization developed by widowed women to offset the financial challenges of, and build community among, widowed women nationwide.

4. *The Life Reentry Institute:* an inner language designed to interrupt the survival-based default setting that is constructed by the human mind to restrict change and thereby remain in a stagnant, self-soothing holding pattern.

It's OK not to feel OK. You are normal, and what you are experiencing is normal. Every single emotion is valid and an important part of the process your body and mind need to eventually move forward. Give yourself grace, listen to your gut, and lean into the natural flow of things.

ACKNOWLEDGMENTS

Writing this memoir has been one of the greatest accomplishments of my life, but also one of the deepest vulnerabilities to overcome. Countless people have supported me through the love, tears, and sorrow I experienced—both during my deep grief and while reliving this book of my life over and over again for more than six years.

To the widows who have experienced this pain before me and for the ones who will follow, and to the countless widowed men and women I've met through this journey: thank you for encouraging me to keep writing, as it is an outlet for grief for many. Thank you for understanding.

To my widow sisters: Tessa, Janelle, and Brianna, thank you for making me feel "normal." I'm so grateful our paths crossed and I have loved watching your own stories unfold.

To my amazing therapists, past and present coworkers who became dear friends, and understanding supervisors I've had the pleasure of working with that kept me sane then and continue to do so now, thank you.

To Shaun: thank you for the extra encouragement to keep going when I didn't think I could. Thank you for the past lessons, both positive and negative. I'll never forget how you helped save my life more than once.

To Jocelyn Carbonara, Jenny Lisk, and Victoria H. Silk: thank you for your guidance, talent, creativity, empowerment, and patience. Thank you for holding me to my truth and supporting me through the writing and publishing journey.

To Bob: thank you for being Wayne's mentor, for being a positive role model in his younger years and beyond. Thank you for your advice and wisdom on deep loss, and for your influence to write my first book after reading yours.

To the Crivitz boys: you know who you all are. Thank you for continuing to include me in your lives and for keeping Wayne's memory alive.

To Wayne's family: Victoria, Christy, Ron, Ruth, and Glenn. Thank you for embracing me as your own and accepting me for who I am.

To my entire family—my sister, cousins, aunts and uncles, niece and nephew, and friends—thank you for loving and supporting me through my pain, whether it be in person or from afar.

To my parents: thank you for the unending support, love, and encouragement through every dark day and into the lighter days that followed.

To Robb: for your endless positive attitude, your patience and encouragement, your ear and your advice, your love and your grace, thank you.

To Wayne: I will forever love and miss you with the power of a million suns. You have changed and touched so many lives. I hope we're making you proud.

ABOUT THE AUTHOR

Six weeks after marrying her best friend of ten years, Cyndi Francois had to start over. Desperately trying to navigate her new reality as a young widow after her husband's unexpected death, she relocated from the Midwestern suburbs to the outskirts of Olympic National Forest in Washington state after a forty-five-thousand-mile national park road trip. She works as a professional copywriter and continues to use nature, writing, and travel to help manifest a full, present life.

Connect with Cyndi at cyndifrancois.com